ORIENTAL COOKERY

ORIENTAL COOKERY

Front cover photograph by Dave Jordan
shows Peking Duck (page 22)

Published 1986 on behalf of
The Boots Company Plc Nottingham England
by Hamlyn Publishing
Bridge House, London Road, Twickenham,
Middlesex, England

ISBN 0 600 32615 2

Set in Gill Sans
by Servis Filmsetting Ltd, Manchester
Printed in Italy

Contents

Useful Facts & Figures

Notes on metrication

In this book quantities are given in metric and Imperial measures. Exact conversion from Imperial to metric measures does not usually give very convenient working quantities and so the metric measures have been rounded off into units of 25 grams. The table below shows the recommended equivalents.

Ounces	Approx g to nearest whole figure	Recommended conversion to nearest unit of 25
1	28	25
2	57	50
3	85	75
4	113	100
5	142	150
6	170	175
7	198	200
8	227	225
9	255	250
10	283	275
11	312	300
12	340	350
13	368	375
14	396	400
15	425	425
16 (1 lb)	454	450
17	482	475
18	510	500
19	539	550
20 (1¼ lb)	567	575

Note When converting quantities over 20 oz first add the appropriate figures in the centre column, then adjust to the nearest unit of 25. As a general guide, 1 kg (1000 g) equals 2.2 lb or about 2 lb 3 oz. This method of conversion gives good results in nearly all cases, although in certain pastry and cake recipes a more accurate conversion is necessary to produce a balanced recipe.

Liquid measures The millilitre has been used in this book and the following table gives a few examples.

Imperial	Approx ml to nearest whole figure	Recommended ml
¼ pint	142	150 ml
½ pint	283	300 ml
¾ pint	425	450 ml
1 pint	567	600 ml
1½ pints	851	900 ml
1¾ pints	992	1000 ml (1 litre)

Spoon measures All spoon measures given in this book are level unless otherwise stated.

Can sizes At present, cans are marked with the exact (usually to the nearest whole number) metric equivalent of the Imperial weight of the contents, so we have followed this practice when giving can sizes.

Oven temperatures

The table below gives recommended equivalents.

	°C	°F	Gas
Very cool	110	225	¼
	120	250	½
Cool	140	275	1
	150	300	2
Moderate	160	325	3
	180	350	4
Moderately hot	190	375	5
	200	400	6
Hot	220	425	7
	230	450	8
Very hot	240	475	9

Note *When making any of the recipes in this book, only follow one set of measures as they are not interchangeable.*

Introduction

At the very mention of the Orient most people conjure up images of exotic travel, hot hazy days, warm long evenings and splendid feasts. For most, however, the experience of eating oriental food probably extends no further than the average Chinese take-away and a selection of spicy meals in the local curry house. Depending on the authenticity and quality of these establishments, the feeling for true oriental cuisine may be completely lost to a commercial necessity to meet the demands of the western fast-food market.

With the increasing availability of exotic foods in the high street supermarkets rather than solely in tucked-away, expensive delicatessens, there is no reason why we should rely on sampling the delights of oriental cooking anywhere other than in our own homes. Apart from the interesting vegetables and herbs, most spices, bottled sauces and flavouring ingredients can be purchased in large towns. If your supermarket does not offer the items you need, then try the health food shops and any small ethnic shops. If you are lucky enough to live near an oriental supermarket, then you will have no problems in buying even the most obscure ingredients. At the end of the book there is a glossary which offers some information on unusual ingredients.

The chapters are divided up by countries and they cover China, Japan, Indonesia, Thailand, Malaysia and India. The range of recipes within each country is often enormous, with regional variations which are long established in culinary tradition.

In this book you will find a selection of dishes which range from the lightest of stir-fries and the most attractive, delicate snacks from Japan to richly spiced recipes and hot, fiery curries. Even though the cuisines of different nations offer their own individual characteristics, there are firm links between the techniques used for cooking and some distinctly similar influences which filter through the recipes. Because of the climate and local produce this is particularly true of the ingredients. It is quite interesting to see how the same ingredients can be taken, prepared, spiced and cooked in ways which produce dishes with quite different textures, colours and flavours.

You will discover these delights as you read through the recipes. If you are familiar with Indian and Chinese cooking, then try some of the foods from other countries and you will appreciate how easy it is to present a superb meal from any one of the oriental nations.

China

When planning a Chinese menu, forget about the three-course theme. For a simple family meal in China, there may be two or three dishes served with plenty of steamed rice or noodles. A soup (or a congee, which is a thick rice soup) may be served first and the rice would follow last. An elaborate feast, on the other hand, would consist of endless courses of different specialities. Generally the small quantities of ingredients used in individual recipes reflects the fact that several dishes would be served. Each person takes a pair of chopsticks and a small bowl and samples a little of every recipe.

Dim sum *are a particularly interesting Chinese speciality. These are snacks, usually served between meals or as a light meal. Steamed Prawn Dumplings and Pork and Prawn Dumplings are just two dim sum recipes which are included for you to try.*

Authentic fish recipes, including Fishball Chop Suey and Fish with Black Beans, are included along with tempting chicken dishes like Quick-fried Chicken. Peking Duck is also included.

You will also find a firepot meal in this chapter. This is the Chinese answer to fondue. A charcoal heated pot full of simmering soup forms the centrepiece and morsels of food cooked in the soup are eaten with a variety of sauces and dips. The meal is concluded by drinking the delicious soup which is used for the cooking. If you do not own a charcoal-heated pot, then a large pan placed over a fondue burner will do just as well.

WUN TUN SOUP

SERVES 6

In China noodles and pasta dishes are almost as important in the diet of the people as rice. The variety of Chinese pasta preparations is endless. I think wun tun soup can be classified as one of half a dozen best–loved Chinese soups. The wun tun dough is made in the same way as pasta for noodles.

Wun Tun Dough:
450 g/1 lb plain flour
2 eggs · water
4 Chinese dried mushrooms
Filling:
675 g/1½ lb pork
salt
175 g/6 oz peeled prawns
100 g/4 oz spring onions
2 teaspoons cornflour
2 teaspoons soy sauce
1 tablespoon brandy
1 teaspoon oil
2 eggs · 3 pints stock

Mix the flour with the eggs, gradually adding enough water to make a pliable dough. Soak the mushrooms in cold water for 3–4 hours.

Mince the pork and season with salt to taste. Drain, scald and shred the mushrooms, discarding stalks. Chop the prawns and spring onions. Cut the dough into 5-cm/2-in squares.

Combine the pork, mushrooms, prawns, and three-quarters of the spring onions, the cornflour, soy sauce, brandy, oil and 1 egg. Blend well. Beat the second egg. Place a teaspoon of the mixture on each square of dough. Fold over, seal with beaten egg and round off the edge of the wun tun. Bring the stock to the boil, put in the wun tun a few at a time, boil fast for 7 minutes, keeping the pan uncovered, and serve.

PORK AND PRAWN STEAMED DUMPLINGS

SERVES 6–8

This recipe and the following one are both varieties of dim sum. They are delicious steamed dumplings served for lunch.

half quantity wun tun dough
(opposite)
225 g/8 oz uncooked, boneless pork
4–6 water chestnuts
1 piece bamboo shoot
50 g/2 oz peeled, cooked prawns
pinch of salt
pinch of sugar
1 teaspoon light soy sauce
pinch of ground ginger
1 tablespoon Chinese wine or
dry sherry

Prepare the dough, knead well, wrap in a damp cloth and leave until the filling is ready. Mince the pork. Chop the water chestnuts and bamboo

Pork and Prawn Steamed Dumplings

shoot. Put the pork in a mixing bowl. Reserve 6–8 prawns for decoration and chop the rest. Combine the pork and chopped prawns with the rest of the ingredients, blend well.

Break off uniform pieces of dough, roll each piece into a thin circle and fray the edges by scraping with the lip of a bowl or saucer. Put 3 teaspoons filling in the centre of each piece of dough and pinch the edges to close around the filling, but leave the top free.

Garnish the top of each dumpling with a whole prawn, put the dumplings in a steamer and steam for 15 minutes. Serve at once.

FIRE KETTLE MEAL

SERVES 6

This is variously known as Mongol hot pot, Japanese hakotsu, Korean sinsullo. The original Chinese variation is called *Ta pin lo*, 'fire kettle'.

Normally the *pin lo* has a charcoal burner – though gas and electric appliances can be bought – and once it is well lit, sprinkle with coarse salt and put in the centre part of the *pin lo*. Stand the *pin lo* on a mat on a concrete slab in the middle of the dining table and fill the outer ring with a clear broth, seasoned to taste.

Arrange your selection of thinly sliced raw food and the assortment of sauces and condiments, all of which are available from Chinese food shops, around the *pin lo*. Each guest has a bowl and spoon, a pair of chopsticks and a long-handled wire ladle, in which they cook their food in the broth.

This is a complete meal, marvellous for a cold winter evening and the ingredients for it can be varied according to what is available or in season. If anyone can face a dessert, serve Chinese toffee apples. And you will need pots and pots of good jasmine tea.

225 g/8 oz chicken breast
2 sole fillets
175 g/6 oz calf's liver or chicken liver
225 g/8 oz lean boneless pork
175 g/6 oz fillet steak
3–4 scallops
225 g/8 oz uncooked prawns
175 g/6 oz white cabbage
175 g/6 oz spinach or lettuce
100 g/4 oz mushrooms
100 g/4 oz canned bamboo shoots
100 g/4 oz transparent noodles
175 g/6 oz bean curd
small bunch of spring onions
1 tablespoon cornflour
2 tablespoons sherry
2 tablespoons water
2 dozen wun tun (page 12)
2-2.5 litres/3½–4 pints chicken stock
Condiments for dipping:
light soy sauce
Chinese vinegar
sesame paste
shrimp sauce
chilli sauce
plum sauce
salt and pepper
6 raw eggs (optional)
6 lettuce 'cups' (optional)

Cut the chicken, sole, liver, pork, steak and scallops into wafer-thin slices. Peel the prawns and cut in half lengthways, remove vein. Cut the cabbage into bite-sized pieces, put in a bowl, cover with boiling water, leave to stand for 5–6 minutes and drain well. Sort and rinse the spinach leaves. Slice the mushrooms and bamboo shoots. Drop the noodles into boiling water, allow to stand for half a minute and drain. Cut the bean curd into squares. Cut the spring onions into 5-cm/2-in lengths, then slice in half lengthways. Blend the cornflour with the sherry and water.

Arrange the chicken, liver, pork and steak in a symmetrical pattern on two dishes. Lay out the sole, prawns and scallop similarly on two other dishes. Sprinkle all these with the cornflour and sherry mixture. Divide all the other sliced ingredients, the wun tun and the noodles also in duplicate dishes – this will enable your guests to help themselves to everything without having to stretch across the hot pot.

Check the stock for seasoning before you pour it into the fire kettle and set it on the table. Arrange all your ingredients and condiments around the fire kettle.

Each diner helps himself to the ingredient he wants, cooks it in the simmering stock, dips it in the condiments of his choice to season and cool it before eating. None of the ingredients needs more than 45–60 seconds to cook through, except the wun tun (see page 12). Usually the noodles are added to cook last of all. If eggs are served, they should be lightly poached in the broth and this is best done by floating the lettuce 'cups' on the surface of the broth, then gently breaking an egg into each one. When all the food has been eaten, cook the noodles in the remaining broth and serve the broth in soup bowls.

STEAMED PRAWN DUMPLINGS

SERVES 6

This is the second of those delicious Chinese steamed dumplings – dim sum, which everyone finds so easy to eat!

100 g/4 oz uncooked, boneless pork
2 spring onions
1 thin slice fresh root ginger
2 tablespoons bamboo shoots
4 uncooked Pacific prawns
1 tablespoon lard
2 tablespoons chopped mushrooms
½ teaspoon sesame oil
pinch of salt
2 teaspoons light soy sauce
¼ teaspoon sugar
1 tablespoon Chinese wine or
dry sherry
½ teaspoon cornflour
2 tablespoons cold water
175 g/6 oz Chinese wheat starch or
plain flour plus extra to roll
175 ml/6 fl oz boiling water

Fish Strips with Celery (page 17)

Mince the pork, finely chop the spring onions and ginger. Cut the bamboo shoots into small dice. Peel, de-vein and chop the prawns.

Heat the lard in a frying pan and toss the pork for 30 seconds. Add the mushrooms, spring onions, ginger, bamboo shoots, prawns and sesame oil. Stir-fry for 30 seconds, season with salt, soy sauce and sugar. Sprinkle in the wine or sherry. Dilute the cornflour in the water, pour over the contents of the frying pan, stir well and turn out the dumpling filling into a bowl.

Adding the water very gradually, mix the wheat starch or flour with the boiling water into a stiff dough. Knead well, sprinkle with flour and roll into a long sausage. Pinch off small pieces of dough of uniform size, roll out into circles 7.5 cm/3 in. in diameter, taking care to fray the edges by scraping them with the lip of a bowl or saucer. Put a good teaspoon of the filling in the middle of each circlet of dough, pinch the edges together forming a semi-circle, steam for 12 minutes and serve piping hot.

FISH STRIPS WITH CELERY

SERVES 4–6

(Illustrated on page 15)

450 g / 1 lb white fish fillet
1 teaspoon salt
1 egg
1½ tablespoon cornflour
1 small head celery
1 tablespoon light soy sauce
1 teaspoon sesame oil
25 g / 1 oz cooked smoked ham
oil for deep frying

Cut the fish first into thin slices, then into thin strips, about 5 cm/2 in long. Beat the salt with the egg. Coat the fish with egg, then with cornflour.

Wash the celery and cut it into matchstick-thin strips. Blanch for 30 seconds in boiling water, then drain. Mix with the soy sauce and sesame oil. Cut the ham into matchsticks.

Heat the oil to 180 C/350 F, or until a day-old cube of bread turns golden in 1 minute.

Deep-fry the fish for 3–4 minutes or until the strips float to the surface. Drain on absorbent kitchen paper. Place the celery mixture in a serving dish and top with the fish. Garnish with the ham and serve.

FISHBALL CHOP SUEY

SERVES 4–6

1 kg / 2 lb white fish fillet
1 egg, beaten
2 teaspoons sesame oil
salt and freshly ground black pepper
2 tablespoons water
½ small green pepper
3 canned water chestnuts
8 dried Chinese mushrooms, soaked and drained
oil for deep frying, plus 3 tablespoons vegetable oil
2 cloves garlic, crushed
50 g / 2 oz bean sprouts
3 slices fresh root ginger
1 tablespoon chutney
15 g / ½ oz cornflour
3 tablespoons chicken stock

Mince the fish, add the egg, half the sesame oil, salt and pepper to taste and the water. Beat well and shape into small balls. Thinly slice the green pepper and water chestnuts. Remove and discard the mushroom stalks.

Heat the oil for deep frying to 180 C/350 F or until a day-old cube of bread turns golden in 1 minute. Deep-fry the fishballs until lightly browned. Drain on absorbent kitchen paper and set aside.

Heat the 3 tablespoons oil in a large frying pan. Add a little salt, the green pepper, water chestnuts, mushrooms, garlic, bean sprouts, ginger and chutney. Stir-fry quickly for 2 minutes. Add the fishballs and continue to cook over a lower heat for 1 minute.

Blend the cornflour with a little water, then mix with the stock and add to the pan. Bring to the boil, stirring, sprinkle with the remaining sesame oil and serve.

Fishball Chop Suey

FISH WITH BLACK BEANS

SERVES 4

450–675 g / 1–1½ lb bream or mullet,
cleaned and descaled
salt
plain flour
1 clove garlic
25 g / 1 oz black soya beans
1 teaspoon soy sauce
1 teaspoon brandy
4 tablespoons oil
1 tablespoon cornflour
300 ml / ½ pint water
4–5 spring onions
15 g / ½ oz cooked lean pork

Make a few shallow incisions at a slant on both sides of the fish. Sprinkle with salt and coat with flour, making it adhere properly.

Chop the garlic finely, scald the black beans and mix with the soy sauce, brandy and garlic. Heat the oil in a large pan and fry the fish until golden. Put on a large serving dish and keep hot.

Pour off surplus oil from pan, fry the black bean mixture for 2 minutes, stirring constantly. Blend the cornflour with the water, add to the pan and cook for 2 minutes, stirring all the time. Cut the spring onions into 5-cm/2-in strips, then with a sharp knife into as many strips lengthways as possible. Add to the pan.

Shred the pork, place in the sauce to heat it.

Pour over the fish, and serve.

LOBSTER WITH RICE NOODLES

SERVES 2

This is a characteristic example of a harmonious combination of sea food with noodles and typically Chinese vegetables. It also makes a small amount of lobster go a long way; if it is served with a couple of other dishes, this quantity will be enough for four.

175 g / 6 oz rice noodles
225 g / 8 oz lobster meat
25 g / 1 oz mushrooms
5-cm / 2-in piece cucumber
50 g / 2 oz canned water chestnuts
50 g / 2 oz canned bamboo shoots
2 celery sticks
½ small onion
75 g / 3 oz bean sprouts
1 tablespoon oil
½ teaspoon salt
1 teaspoon sugar
1 tablespoon soy sauce
1.15 litres / 2 pints chicken stock

Put the noodles in a bowl, cover with hot water and leave to stand for 30 minutes. Dice the lobster meat. Slice the mushrooms, cucumber, water chestnuts, bamboo shoots, celery and onion. Sort and rinse and drain the bean sprouts.

Heat the oil in a large saucepan and sauté the lobster for 1 minute. Add the salt, sugar, soy sauce and enough stock to cover. Cook for 1 minute, add the drained noodles, cook for 2 minutes, and serve.

STRANGE-FLAVOUR CHICKEN

SERVES 4

4 chicken thighs
25 g/1 oz sesame seeds
1½ teaspoons sesame oil
1½ tablespoons soy sauce
2 teaspoons caster sugar
1 tablespoon vinegar
1 teaspoon chilli sauce
¼ teaspoon freshly ground black pepper
6–8 large spring onions

Cook the chicken joints in a saucepan of boiling water for 5 minutes, then reduce the heat and simmer for 15 minutes, or until the chicken is cooked through. Drain and cool for 10 minutes. Chop each of the thighs into three or four pieces. Alternatively, cut the meat off the bones and slice into four pieces.

Stir-fry the sesame seeds gently in a dry pan over very low heat until they are just turning golden and beginning to crackle. Reserve one-third of the seeds and pound the rest to a powder, slowly

Strange-flavour Chicken

adding the sesame oil to make sesame paste. Mix this paste with the soy sauce, sugar, vinegar, chilli sauce and pepper.

Slice the spring onions and pile them in the centre of a serving dish. Overlap the pieces of chicken around the edge of the dish. Pour the sesame paste mixture evenly over the chicken and sprinkle the crispy, dry sesame seeds on top before serving. The sweet-sour flavour of the sesame paste, pepped up with the chilli sauce, perfectly complements the cold chicken.

CHICKEN WITH WALNUTS

SERVES 4

100 g/4 oz mushrooms
225 g/8 oz uncooked chicken meat
1 tablespoon soy sauce
1 tablespoon brandy
1 teaspoon cornflour
salt
1 tablespoon oil
1 clove garlic, crushed
50 g/2 oz celery
1 tablespoon oyster sauce
100 g/4 oz walnuts
150 ml/¼ pint water
2–3 spring onions

Cut the mushrooms in 5-mm/¼-in slices. Dice the chicken and combine it with the soy sauce, brandy, cornflour and salt to taste. Heat the oil in a pan and brown the garlic in it.

Discard the garlic and fry the chicken briskly for 1½–2 minutes without allowing it to brown. Slice the celery. Add the oyster sauce, mushrooms and celery to the chicken. Simmer for 5 minutes, stirring constantly. Add the walnuts and water. Simmer for 2 minutes. Slice the spring onions, sprinkle them over the dish and serve.

Variation:

Chicken with Almonds Proceed as above, substituting blanched almonds for walnuts, but whereas the walnuts are added to the dish shortly before it is served, the almonds should be fried in an oiled pan with a little salt added. The frying of almonds requires great care as they tend to burn very quickly. They must be stirred constantly and removed as soon as they turn golden. Drain on kitchen paper then add to dish as described for Chicken with Walnuts.

SALT-BURIED CHICKEN

SERVES 6

1 (1-kg/2-lb) chicken
1 tablespoon soy sauce
6 spring onions
4 teaspoons chopped fresh root
ginger
1 teaspoon salt
2 tablespoons cherry brandy
2.75 kg/6 lb coarse grain salt
Dip
2 tablespoons chopped spring onions
2 teaspoons chopped fresh root
ginger
1 teaspoon salt
4 tablespoons chicken stock
2 teaspoons salad oil

Clean the chicken thoroughly and dip it quickly in boiling water. Take out, drain the bird then pull and stretch it. Dip in boiling water again. Dry the chicken thoroughly and rub the outside with the soy sauce, then hang it up to dry for 3 hours.

Wash the spring onions and crush them with the side of a knife, so that they are slightly bruised. Put the ginger and spring onions in a bowl and add the 1 teaspoon salt and the cherry brandy. Mix them together. When the chicken is dry, stuff it with this mixture.

Heat the coarse grain salt in a large cast-iron pot. When quite hot, make a hole in the middle and bury the chicken in the salt. Cover the pot. Place it over low heat for 10 minutes. Remove from the heat and let stand for 10 minutes. Repeat this process twice more during the space of 1 hour. Alternatively, the pot can be placed in a moderate oven (160 C, 325 F, gas 3) for 1¼ hours. Remove the chicken from the salt and chop the bird into 1.5 × 3-cm/¾ × 1½-in pieces, discarding the stuffing.

Arrange the pieces of chicken on a heated plate in a spreadeagle pattern. Make the dip by boiling the spring onions, ginger, salt, chicken stock and salad oil together for 3–4 seconds. The diner usually dips the chicken in this mixture at the table before eating.

QUICK-FRIED CHICKEN

SERVES 2–4

This is another dish of successfully contrasting textures. The sweet pepper and chilli peppers give the chicken a delicious piquant flavour.

2 large boneless chicken breasts
50 g/2 oz canned bamboo shoots
1 small red pepper
1 spring onion
2 dried red chillies
1 teaspoon salt
1 egg
1 tablespoon cornflour
3 tablespoons vegetable oil
25 g/1 oz lard
4 tablespoons chicken stock
1 tablespoon dry sherry
1 tablespoon light soy sauce
1 teaspoon sesame oil

Cut the chicken into 5-mm/$\frac{1}{4}$-in cubes. Cut the bamboo shoots and the deseeded red pepper into similar-sized pieces. Slice the spring onion into

Quick-fried Chicken

5-mm/$\frac{1}{4}$-in pieces. Chop the chillies and discard the seeds.

Place the diced chicken in a bowl. Add the salt and rub it into the chicken. Beat the egg then whisk in the cornflour until smooth. Coat the chicken in the cornflour mixture. Heat the oil in a large frying pan and stir-fry the chicken for 1$\frac{1}{2}$ minutes. Remove the chicken and discard any remaining oil. Add the lard to the pan. Stir-fry the bamboo shoots, red pepper and the chillies over high heat for 2 minutes.

Mix the chicken stock with the sherry and add to the pan, together with the soy sauce and sesame oil. Stir-fry gently for 30 seconds. Add the pieces of chicken and continue to stir-fry for another 30 seconds. Transfer to a heated dish and serve.

STIR-FRIED CHICKEN WITH SOY JAM

SERVES 2–4

1 (175-g/6-oz) chicken breast
1 egg white
1 tablespoon water
1 tablespoon cornflour
½ teaspoon ground ginger
40 g/ 1½ oz lard
1½ tablespoons brown soy jam
1 teaspoon caster sugar
1 tablespoon dry sherry
½ teaspoon soft brown sugar

Strip the chicken meat from the bone and soak it in cold water for 1 hour. Drain, dry and cut into 1-cm/ ½-in cubes. Mix the egg white with the water in a bowl. Beat in the cornflour to make a thin batter. Add the chicken and coat evenly with your fingers.

Heat two-thirds of the lard in a frying pan over a low heat. Add the chicken, separating the cubes until they are well spread out, and stir-fry slowly for 1 minute. Remove the chicken and set aside.

Discard the lard from the pan and add the remaining lard. When melted, add the soy jam and stir until all moisture has evaporated (when the sizzling has almost stopped). Add the ginger, caster sugar, sherry and brown sugar, and stir into a creamy paste. Replace the chicken. Stir and mix with the rich 'jam' over high heat for about 10–12 seconds, or until the chicken is glistening brown. If desired, add a little extra lard. Let it melt completely and give everything a last stir. This adds to the general smoothness. Transfer to a medium-sized flat plate and serve with rice.

PEKING DUCK

SERVES 4–6

(Illustrated on front cover)

1 (1.75–2.75-kg/4–6-lb) oven-ready duck
4 tablespoons dry sherry
4 tablespoons soy sauce
½ teaspoon five-spice powder
Pancakes
175 g/6 oz plain flour
25 g/ 1 oz lard
150 ml/¼ pint boiling water
sesame oil for cooking
To serve
½ cucumber
bunch of spring onions
hoisin sauce

Have ready a very large pan of boiling water, plunge the duck into it and bring back to the boil. Drain thoroughly and dry the duck with absorbent kitchen paper. Leave to dry overnight.

Mix the sherry, soy sauce and spice, then rub this all over the inside and outside of the duck. Place on a rack over a roasting tin and cook in a moderately hot oven (200 C, 400 F, gas 6) for about 1½ hours or until golden and crisp. Baste frequently with the soy sauce mixture during cooking.

Make the pancakes while the duck roasts. Sift the flour into a bowl. Melt the lard in the boiling water, then mix into the flour to make a smooth dough. Cut the dough into 20 small portions; keep the dough covered while rolling the pancakes. Roll the dough on a floured surface to make small thin pancakes, brush lightly with sesame oil and sandwich them in pairs, oiled sides together. Cook the pairs on a hot griddle, turning once until very lightly browned on the outside. Separate the pancakes and cook the second side of each very briefly. Place in a bamboo steamer or on a covered plate over a saucepan of boiling water.

Finely shred the cucumber and spring onions, then put in iced water to make the pieces as crisp as possible. Drain well.

The skin and meat is removed from the duck and cut into fine pieces. Each person takes a pancake and spreads a little hoisin sauce on it, then adds duck, cucumber and spring onions. The pancakes are folded and eaten at once.

DOUBLE-COOKED PORK

SERVES 4–6

Double-cooked pork is said to have been first invented in Szechwan, although it is now popular throughout China. It is not exactly a delicacy, but because of the attractive green and red-brown colour combination, it is sometimes included at a dinner party. This recipe comes from the Fei Yung Dining Rooms, Chengtu.

1 kg/2 lb chump end or loin of pork
1 small leek
1 tablespoon fermented black beans,
soaked for 1 hour in cold water
15 g/½ oz lard
1½ teaspoons caster sugar
1 tablespoon soy sauce
1 teaspoon chilli sauce
2 teaspoons plum sauce or hoisin
sauce

Boil the pork in water to cover for 20 minutes. Drain and cool for 30 minutes. Remove the rind and cut the pork into 2.5 × 3-cm/1 × 1½-in slices.

Double-cooked Pork

Each slice should have both lean meat and fat. Trim the leek so that there are equal parts of green and white, then cut it into 3-cm/1½-in lengths. Mash the fermented beans into a paste.

Heat the lard in a frying pan. Add the pork and cook for 2 minutes over low heat. Add the sugar, soy sauce, chilli sauce and plum sauce or hoisin sauce, and turn the heat to high. Stir-fry for 20 seconds, add the leeks and continue to stir-fry for 1½ minutes. Serve at once.

SWEET AND SOUR PORK

SERVES 4–6

This basic sweet and sour sauce can be used for a great many foods: chicken, duck, spare ribs, bream, sea bass, trout, plaice, lobster, prawns, scallops, mixed vegetables, and by following this recipe you will be able to ring the changes.

450 g/1 lb boneless pork
salt
1 egg, beaten
50 g/2 oz cornflour
lard or oil for deep frying
For sweet and sour sauce:
2 slices canned pineapple
2 teaspoons oil
pinch of ground ginger
2 tablespoons vinegar
1½ tablespoons sugar
½ tablespoon tomato sauce
2 teaspoons cornflour
1½ teaspoons soy sauce
1 teaspoon brandy
300 ml/½ pint water
50 g/2 oz spring onions

Choose a piece of pork with both lean meat and fat. Skin it and cut into 2½-cm/1-in cubes, season with salt. Dip the cubes into the beaten egg, then into the cornflour and deep fry in the lard or oil. The pork is cooked when it rises to the surface and acquires a lovely golden colour. Drain, heap on a dish and serve covered with sweet and sour sauce prepared in the following manner.

Dice the pineapple, then fry in the oil sprinkled with ginger. Mix the vinegar, sugar, tomato sauce, cornflour, soy sauce and brandy together. Stir, blend in the water, and add the mixture to the fried pineapple. Simmer gently for 5 minutes, stirring all the time. If the sauce becomes too thick, add a little more water. Slice the spring onions, add to sauce, stir, pour sauce over the pork and serve.

YELLOW FLOWER MEAT

SERVES 4

(Illustrated on page 31)

A popular dish with the people of Peking and the north, this is a scrambled omelette cooked with some shredded meat and one or two other ingredients.

4 eggs
½ teaspoon salt
100 g/4 oz lean boneless pork
8 dried Chinese mushrooms, soaked and drained
3 spring onions
4 tablespoons vegetable oil
1 tablespoon soy sauce
2 tablespoons chicken stock
1 teaspoon caster sugar
1 tablespoon dry sherry
1 teaspoon sesame oil

Beat the eggs in a bowl for a few seconds and add the salt. Shred the pork into matchstick-thin strips. Cut the mushrooms into thin strips or small pieces. Cut the spring onions into very thin slices. Heat half the oil in a frying pan and add the beaten egg. Reduce the heat (so that none of the egg burns) and just before the egg sets completely, scramble it slightly. Remove from the pan and set aside.

Add the remaining oil to the frying pan and turn the heat to high. Add the pork, mushrooms and spring onions. Sauté for 2 minutes, then add the soy sauce, stock and sugar. Cook for a further 30–40 seconds. Add the scrambled egg, sherry and sesame oil. Stir gently to mix all the ingredients. Serve on a heated dish.

Sweet and Sour Pork

BEEF IN OYSTER SAUCE

SERVES 6

Although pork is the meat which figures mainly on Chinese menus, beef is used in some areas and there are hundreds of recipes for preparing it.

450 g / 1 lb rump steak
2 teaspoons cornflour
$\frac{1}{2}$ teaspoon sugar
1 teaspoon soy sauce
pinch of salt
75 g / 3 oz canned bamboo shoots
25 g / 1 oz chives
7 g / $\frac{1}{4}$ oz fresh root ginger
6 spring onions
1 tablespoon peanut oil
1 tablespoon oyster sauce
2 tablespoons water

Cut the meat into thin strips. Put in a bowl, sprinkle with 1 teaspoon of the cornflour, the sugar, soy sauce and salt and mix well.

Cut the bamboo shoots into thin strips. Cut the chives into 2.5-cm/1-in lengths. Slice the ginger and onions very finely.

Heat the oil in a frying pan, add the ginger and onion and fry for 2 minutes. Add beef and fry, stirring all the time, for 2 minutes. Add the bamboo shoots, stir carefully, cook for 1 minute, sprinkle in the chives and blend in the oyster sauce.

Blend the remaining cornflour with the water to make a smooth paste. Stir into pan, bring to the boil and cook for 1 minute to thicken the sauce. Serve immediately with boiled rice.

CRISP-FRIED BEEF

SERVES 4

225 g / 8 oz lean frying steak
1 tablespoon chopped onion
1 tablespoon finely chopped fresh root ginger
1 tablespoon sweet sherry
1 tablespoon sesame oil
1 egg
25 g / 1 oz plain flour
15 g / $\frac{1}{2}$ oz cornflour
150 ml / $\frac{1}{4}$ pint vegetable oil
1 teaspoon salt
1 teaspoon freshly ground black pepper

Cut the beef across the grain into 1 × 2.5-cm/$\frac{1}{2}$ × 1-in slices. Place in a bowl and add the onion, ginger, sherry with 2 teaspoons of the sesame oil. Mix well with the fingertips and set aside to marinate for 30 minutes. Beat the egg then stir in the flour and cornflour. Pour the mixture over the beef and mix well.

Heat the vegetable oil in a large frying pan. When hot, add the beef, separating the pieces and spreading them out. Stir-fry gently over high heat for 2 minutes.

Remove the frying pan from the heat for 1 minute, letting the beef simmer at the reduced heat. Replace the pan over high heat and stir-fry for 1 minute. Remove the pan from the heat again and leave for 1 minute, then repeat this process once more. This method of frying prevents the oil from overheating but at the same time ensures that the meat is very crisp when cooked.

Drain the beef thoroughly and place on a heated serving dish. Sprinkle with the remaining sesame oil. Mix the salt and pepper and divide between two small dishes or saucers to use as a dip.

SLICED LAMB HOT SCRAMBLED WITH ONION

SERVES 4

This dish, from the Peking Municipal Public Service Bureau Catering Department, is another favourite of the people. It is such a tasty and aromatic dish that, although it is served in every dining hall and transport café, it is also found on top tables, in elegant households or on party menus.

175 g/6 oz lean lamb, cut from the leg
1 tablespoon cornflour
1 tablespoon water
50 g/2 oz spring onions or shallots
3 cloves garlic
3 tablespoons oil
1 tablespoon soy sauce
½ teaspoon salt
1 tablespoon sherry
1 teaspoon sesame oil

Cut the lamb across the grain into thin 5 × 2.5-cm/ 2 × 1-in slices. Mix the cornflour with the water,

Sliced Lamb Hot Scrambled with Onion

then mix the paste with the meat. Cut the spring onions or shallots into 5-cm/2-in pieces, including the green part, and put to one side. Crush the garlic.

Heat 2 tablespoons of the oil in a large frying pan over medium heat and stir-fry the lamb gently for 2 minutes. Remove the meat and put aside. Add the remaining 1 tablespoon oil to the pan and fry the onion and crushed garlic for 2 minutes. Return the meat to the pan and add the soy sauce, salt and sherry, and scramble-fry over high heat for 1 minute. Add the sesame oil immediately before serving.

Since this is a mixed, scrambled dish, no garnishing or decoration is necessary. It should, however, be very neatly and carefully poured on to a well-heated plain or decorated dish and eaten immediately. This is a great dish for those who appreciate the aromatic qualities of quick-fried garlic and onion.

PEKING SLICED LAMB HOT-POT

SERVES 4–6

This method of cooking is the same as for the Fire Kettle Meal (see page 14).

1 kg/2 lb lamb (about 225 g/8 oz for
each serving)
1 (450-g/1-lb) Chinese cabbage
100 g/4 oz spinach
1.75 litres/3 pints chicken stock
100 g/4 oz transparent noodles
Dips
soy sauce
sesame oil
sesame paste
vinegar
chilli sauce
tomato sauce
shrimp sauce
mustard
sugar and crushed garlic
ground coriander
spring onion

Cut the lamb into 18 × 5-cm/7 × 2½-in paper-thin slices and allow about 15 pieces to each of four or six small plates. Shred the cabbage and cut away the thicker stalks of the spinach.

Pour the stock into a fire kettle or pan and place over the heat. As soon as the stock starts to boil furiously, add about a quarter of the prepared vegetables and the noodles. Within 1–2 minutes it will reboil. Cook for about 10 minutes, then serve the noodles and vegetables in soup bowls.

Each person puts his own slices of the meat in the pan to cook. Meanwhile the diner mixes his dip in the empty bowl in front of him. The dip can be a mixture of some or all of the ingredients listed above. The diner can even have two bowls of different dips for the meat.

HOT-FRIED KIDNEY

SERVES 4

(Illustrated on page 33)

350 g/12 oz pig's kidneys
1½ tablespoons cornflour
1 tablespoon water
1½ tablespoons dry sherry
½ teaspoon salt
1 tablespoon caster sugar
1 tablespoon vinegar
1 tablespoon soy sauce
2 tablespoons chicken stock
3 spring onions
1 dried red chilli
1 small leek
4–5 tablespoons vegetable oil
2 cloves garlic
3 slices fresh root ginger
¼ teaspoon chilli powder
freshly ground black pepper

Cut each kidney in half, then remove and discard the core. Slash with criss-cross cuts 5 mm/¼ in apart and two-thirds through the kidneys. Cut into 1.5 × 2.5-cm/¾ × 1-in pieces. Blend half the cornflour with the water, the sherry and salt. Thoroughly coat the kidney pieces in this mixture. In a separate bowl, mix the remaining cornflour, the sugar, vinegar, soy sauce and chicken stock. Set aside. Cut the spring onions into 1-cm/½-in pieces. Remove and discard the seeds from the chilli. Cut the leek into 1-cm/½-in strips.

Heat the oil in a frying pan until very hot. Add the kidney, spreading the pieces evenly, sauté for 15 seconds and then put aside. Discard the excess oil. In the same pan, sauté the chilli for 1 minute and discard. Crush the garlic, then stir-fry the spring onion, leek, garlic, ginger and chilli powder for 20 seconds. Add the kidney pieces and stir-fry for 10 seconds. Gradually add the vinegar mixture. Pour this slowly from the bowl into the pan. Stir-fry the kidney gently for 15 seconds. Add pepper to taste and serve immediately.

Peking Sliced Lamb Hot-pot

VEGETARIAN NOODLES

SERVES 4–6

This method of cooking vegetarian noodles is well established in Szechwan. Originally, it was a popular dish of the people, who often prepared it to entertain their friends and relatives on special occasions. It was also served from mobile carrier stalls which were carried on shoulder-poles, with a charcoal cooker and washbasin at one end and the bowls, utensils, chopsticks and spoons at the other.

3 tablespoons sesame paste
1 tablespoon sesame oil
2 tablespoons wine vinegar
1 tablespoon caster sugar
2 tablespoons soy sauce
1 teaspoon chilli sauce
freshly ground black pepper
450 g/1 lb Chinese egg noodles
2 tablespoons finely chopped spring onion tops
1 tablespoon finely chopped garlic

Mix together the sesame paste, sesame oil, vinegar, sugar, soy sauce, chilli sauce and pepper to taste. Divide the mixture between four or six separate bowls.

Boil the noodles for 15 minutes. Drain and while the noodles are steaming hot, divide them into portions and place on top of the mixture in the bowls. Sprinkle the noodles with the chopped spring onion tops and garlic. Each diner uses his own chopsticks to toss and mix the noodles with the ingredients and seasonings.

Vegetarian Noodles

MIXED VEGETABLE STIR-FRY

SERVES 4

Vegetables form an important part of the Chinese diet. Several vegetables might be eaten at every meal and Chinese vegetable cookery is a highly developed art. This is a delicious dish of Chinese mixed vegetables. Once the mushrooms have been treated, it takes only a few minutes to prepare.

3 Chinese dried mushrooms
300 ml/½ pint hot chicken stock
225 g/8 oz canned bamboo shoot
4 water chestnuts
1 clove garlic
1 tablespoon peanut oil
1 small onion
½ teaspoon salt
¼ teaspoon freshly ground black pepper
½ teaspoon soy sauce
1 teaspoon cornflour
1 tablespoon cold water

Soak the mushrooms overnight. Bring half the stock to the boil, add the mushrooms, simmer for

Yellow Flower Meat (page 25)

10 minutes and drain. Remove the stalks and slice the mushrooms. Thinly slice the bamboo shoots and the water chestnuts.

Crush the garlic and fry in the oil until it browns lightly, and discard. Roughly chop the onion and toss it in the garlic-flavoured oil for 10–15 seconds. Add bamboo shoots, water chestnuts and mushrooms. Cook, stirring, for half a minute.

Add the remaining stock. Season with salt, pepper and the soy sauce. Bring to the boil. Mix the cornflour with the cold water to make a smooth paste. Blend it into the pan and bring to the boil. Cook, stirring, for 2 minutes. Transfer to a heated dish and serve immediately with boiled rice or noodles.

Variations
Try any of the following combinations of vegetables in the stir-fry. Cauliflower, water chestnuts and mushrooms. French beans, cabbage heart, broccoli and onion. Turnips, carrots, celery and leeks. Chinese cabbage, celery hearts and asparagus or snow peas. Spinach, bamboo shoots, mushrooms and bean sprouts.

PINE-FLOWER MEAT SOUFFLÉ OMELETTE

SERVES 4-6

6 eggs
25 g/1 oz plain flour
1 teaspoon salt
100 g/4 oz lean pork
2 spring onions
25 g/1 oz dried Chinese mushrooms,
soaked and drained
25 g/1 oz bamboo shoots
1 teaspoon caster sugar
1 tablespoon soy sauce
¼ teaspoon five-spice powder
75 g/3 oz lard
2 tablespoons chopped parsley
1 tablespoon dry sherry

Separate the eggs. Whisk the whites for 2 minutes or until nearly stiff. Fold in the yolks, flour and salt. Finely chop the pork and spring onions. Slice the mushrooms and bamboo shoots into matchstick-thin strips. Place the pork, spring onions, mushrooms, bamboo shoots, sugar, soy sauce and five-spice powder in a bowl. Mix well.

Heat 15 g/2 oz of the lard in a small pan. Add the pork mixture and stir-fry for 3 minutes. Remove from the heat and set aside. Place half the remaining lard in a large frying pan over very low heat. When the lard has melted, add half the egg mixture, which will spread into a 15-cm/6-in diameter circle. When the egg has set, gently put the cooked pork mixture into the centre.

After 1 minute of cooking over low heat, pour the remainder of the egg mixture over the filling. Heat the remaining lard in a small saucepan until very hot and pour it over the soft egg mixture. Sprinkle the parsley over the omelette then pour over the sherry. Cook for 30 seconds without stirring. Then gradually lift one side of the omelette to drain away the lard. Use a large spatula to lift the omelette on to a heated serving plate and serve immediately.

Pine-flower Meat Soufflé Omelette

BAMBOO SHOOTS WITH PICKLED CABBAGE

SERVES 4–6

This recipe uses the popular Szechwan salted cabbage to give a highly savoury flavour to the bamboo and chicken. It is ideal to accompany rice and meat dishes.

675 g/ 1½ lb winter bamboo shoots
40 g/ 1½ oz pickled cabbage
25 g/ 1 oz lard
6 tablespoons chicken stock
1 teaspoon salt
2 tablespoons dry sherry
1½ teaspoons cornflour
1½ tablespoons water
15 g/ ½ oz chicken fat

Remove and discard the outer layers of the bamboo shoots and reserve the softer hearts. Slice these lengthways into 5 mm × 1-cm/¼ × ½-in wide strips and then cut into 3 × 5-cm/1½ × 2-in segments. Finely chop the pickled cabbage.

Hot-fried Kidney (page 28)

Heat the lard in a frying pan. When hot, add the bamboo shoots and stir-fry for 1 minute over medium heat. Add the cabbage and stir-fry for 1 minute.

Pour in the chicken stock, salt and sherry. Simmer for 3 minutes. Blend the cornflour with the water until smooth, then add to the pan, stirring all the time. Continue to stir-fry gently until the mixture boils and thickens. Add the chicken fat in small pieces before transferring to a serving dish.

Note: Winter bamboo shoots are available from specialist oriental supermarkets. Alternatively, you can substitute canned bamboo shoots in this recipe.

Japan

Japanese cuisine is unique in its delicacy and it is also surprising in its simplicity. The light cooking techniques which are employed complement perfectly the current concern about healthy eating.

Red meat does not feature largely in the Japanese diet and where it is used, only prime cuts are taken and trimmed of all fat. Sukiyaki is one example of a dish which uses beef but it is a comparatively modern dish in the realms of Japanese cuisine.

When most people think of Japanese food they think of raw fish. Fish and shellfish of all types feature prominently in Japanese cooking. The ingredients are usually the freshest possible and the one dish which is very well known is sashimi. Carefully prepared, often finely sliced and always artistically presented, the fish is served uncooked in sashimi, with condiments and garnishes.

Tempura, another famous speciality, is included in this chapter and, of course, no selection of Japanese recipes would be complete without sushi. These are delicate, tempting bites prepared from Japanese rice, nori (a Japanese seaweed) and other ingredients like smoked salmon for example. To sample these and other delights of the Japanese culinary art just try some of the recipes which follow.

CUSTARD SOUP

SERVES 4

This is perhaps the most famous of Japanese custard soups. Japanese soups are generally served in individual covered bowls. Lacquer ones are ideal for serving hot soups. When the lid is put on, a vacuum is created and this helps to keep the soup hot. Before removing the lid, the bowl should be squeezed lightly to release the lid.

> *100 g/4 oz uncooked chicken*
> *Japanese soy sauce*
> *2 dried mushrooms*
> *12 gingko nuts*
> *1.15 litres/2 pints Japanese stock*
> *(page 36)*
> *salt*
> *4 eggs*
> *½ Japanese fish cake*
> *12 large sprigs watercress*
> *600 ml/1 pint water*
> *1 tablespoon vinegar*
> *8 peeled cooked prawns*
> *2 thin slices lemon*

Slice the chicken, sprinkle with 1 tablespoon soy sauce and leave to stand for 15 minutes. Soak the mushrooms in cold water for 10 minutes to soften; trim off stalks. Shell and boil the gingko nuts to remove outer layer of flesh. Heat the stock, season with salt and soy sauce to taste. Leave to cool.

Beat the eggs, then whisk them into the cold stock and strain. Cut the Japanese fish cake diagonally into neat slices. Tie the watercress in bundles of three sprigs, dip into hot water for a second, then trim the ends to a uniform length.

Divide the chicken, mushrooms, gingko nuts, fish cake and the prawns equally between four bowls and decorate with the watercress. Add half a slice of lemon to each bowl, fill with the egg and stock mixture, cover and put in a steamer (or bain-marie). Steam for 15–20 minutes or until set. Serve in the same covered bowls, placed on folded paper napkins.

Sashimi (page 39)

JAPANESE STOCK

The Japanese use this stock, known as *dashi*, as the basis for other stocks, soups, sauces and dressings. It is very easy to make and the ingredients are available in shops specialising in oriental produce. The two vital ingredients are *konbu*, seaweed, and *katsuobushi*, bonito fish fillets, cut into shavings. As an alternative a strained, light fish stock may be used.

7g/¼ oz konbu seaweed
1.15 litres/2 pints water
30g/1¼ oz bonito fish shavings
pinch of salt

Put the seaweed in a pan with the water, heat and bring slowly to the boil. Remove from heat as soon as the water boils. Add the bonito fish shavings, reheat and again remove from the heat at the first sign of boiling. Season, allow to stand for 10 minutes, then strain and use as required.

TOMATO AND EGG SANDWICH

SERVES 6

Known as *Hakata*, this is a favourite Japanese hors d'oeuvre.

1–2 large tomatoes
2 eggs
pinch of salt
1 generous teaspoon sugar
1 tablespoon cooked peas
6 slices bread

Dip the tomatoes into boiling water for a moment to loosen the skin, peel and cut into 5-mm/¼-in slices.

Beat the eggs, add the salt and sugar. Pour into a non-stick pan and scramble until set. Beat well to give a smooth paste consistency. Remove from heat and add the peas.

Use the scrambled egg and tomato slices to make two triple-decker sandwiches with the tomato on top of egg between 2 slices of bread. Wrap the sandwiches in a dampened napkin and put under a weight. Leave for at least 30 minutes.

To serve, unwrap the sandwiches, trim off the crusts and cut into small dainty sandwiches.

SUSHI

The base for sushi is Japanese rice which is cooked and dressed with slightly sweetened Japanese rice vinegar. The rice is then moulded with a variety of other ingredients.

Allow 350 g/12 oz Japanese rice to serve four. Cook the rice following the instructions for Japanese Rice (right). Mix 4 tablespoons rice vinegar with 25 g/1 oz caster sugar and a generous pinch of salt. Immediately the rice is cooked turn it into a large bowl. Pour in the rice vinegar mixture and toss the grains to mix it in. Fan the rice to cool it quickly as you mix in the vinegar. The rice is now ready to mould. Keep your hands damp to prevent the rice sticking. Try some or all of the following suggestions, remembering always to use the freshest of seafood.

Arrange the prepared Sushi on a platter, adding some cooked large prawns which are peeled but with tails left on. If you like make a rolled omelette to serve with the sushi. Cook a thin layer of beaten egg in a pan until almost set on top, then roll up tightly and pour more egg into the pan. When the second omelette is almost set, roll the omelette back again over it. Repeat once more, remove from the pan and cut into slices. Garnish the slices with strips of nori or smoked salmon.

Squid Sushi Use very fresh squid. Remove the head and tentacles, discard the fine clear quill which runs down the length of the body. Wash and dry on absorbent kitchen paper, then slit the prepared squid and roll it round spoonfuls of the prepared rice. Wrap a small strip of nori round the squid.

Smoked Salmon Sushi Top fine slices of smoked salmon with rice, moulding it together well, then roll it up tightly.

Smoked Trout Cut smoked trout into fine slices and top with rice, then roll up lightly.

Nori Sushi Wave fine sheets of nori (dried seaweed) over a gas flame or electric ring until it changes colour. Top with rice. Put a fine stick (julienne shaped) of cucumber, spring onion or smoked salmon at one end and roll up. Use a sharp wetted knife to slice the sushi.

JAPANESE RICE

For Japanese rice dishes allow $1\frac{1}{4}$ cups water to 1 cup rice. There is an alternative method: shake the rice evenly over the bottom of the pan and add water to reach the level of 2.5–3 cm / 1–$1\frac{1}{4}$ in above the rice.

The Japanese have a special utensil for cooking rice, called a *kama*, and the rice is cooked (as is much of the food) on a charcoal burning stove or *hibachi*. With gas and electric cookers, a heavy-based saucepan with a lid, or a double saucepan, is best.

There are two popular Japanese methods for boiling rice. The preparation is the same in both cases. An hour before cooking, wash the rice until the water runs clear, and leave to drain. Place in a deep saucepan, add the water and proceed as follows.

Place the covered pan over a high heat and bring to the boil. Reduce the heat to very low and simmer for 3 minutes. Raise the heat and bring to the boil again, gradually lowering the heat as the water evaporates. There should be no water left at the end of 18–20 minutes. Raise the heat to its fullest extent for a couple of seconds before removing the pan from the stove. Allow to stand for 6–7 minutes without removing the lid. Serve.

Alternatively, place the covered pan over a high heat and bring to the boil. Reduce the heat to moderate and simmer for 10 minutes. Reduce the heat to very low and simmer for another 10 minutes. Turn off the heat, but leave the pan to stand for a further 10 minutes before uncovering it.

Whichever method you use, never take the lid off the pan while the rice is cooking because the loss of steam affects the cooking process. The rice is ready when all the water has been absorbed. It is also important to let the rice 'rest' for about 10 minutes after cooking, without removing the lid. This prevents the rice from becoming glutinous and gives it an attractive 'risen' look.

Sushi (opposite)

BEEF SUKIYAKI

SERVES 4

Sukiyaki must be the best known Japanese dish in the West. The word means 'roasted on a plough'. The Japanese pronounce it *ski-ya-keh* and it is a reminder of ancient times, when soldiers cooked meat on a plough share, or in a helmet.

It is an excellent dish for a party, because it gives the hostess a chance to serve a delicious and festive-looking meal with very little cooking. All the cooking, in fact, is done in batches at table, in front of the guests and *sukiyaki* is eaten as it is cooked.

The decorative and colourful arrangement of the ingredients is a pleasure to look at and the smell and sight of food sizzling in the pan on the table is guaranteed to stimulate the appetite.

450 g / 1 lb best rump steak
175 g / 6 oz onions
225 g / 8 oz leaf spinach
1 head crisp lettuce
450 g / 1 lb bean curd
16 mushrooms
300 ml / $\frac{1}{2}$ pint Japanese stock (page 36)
8 tablespoons Japanese soy sauce
6 tablespoons sugar
2 tablespoons sake (or dry sherry)
1 tablespoon lard or suet
boiled rice
4 raw eggs

Slice the beef as thin as bacon rashers. Cut the onions at an angle into bite-sized pieces. Pick over the spinach leaves, tear the lettuce leaves into pieces with your fingers. Cut the bean curd into squares. Remove the mushroom stalks. Heat the stock, and soy sauce, sugar and sake.

Arrange the beef and vegetables on a large dish in separate groups and place near the stove. Bear in mind that a pleasing presentation of these raw materials is a part of your table setting.

Grease a frying pan with lard or suet, lay half the beef in it in one layer, brown and turn. Move the beef to one side, moisten with stock mixture. Put in half the spinach, onion, lettuce, bean curd and mushrooms, but keep all the ingredients in separate groups. Turn carefully, so as not to transform the contents of the pan into a mixed fry.

Do not overcook the vegetables. As soon as they are done, taste for seasoning, adding more of the stock mixture if necessary. The characteristic flavour of *sukiyaki* is a pleasant combination of sweet and sharp.

Serve the beef as soon as it is cooked, accompa-nied by a small bowl of boiled rice for each guest. Serve 1 raw egg for each person in an individual bowl.

The diners help themselves to whatever they like and dip the scalding hot ingredients into slightly beaten egg, which serves both as a dressing and to cool the food to just the right temperature to be enjoyed. Prepare to cook the second helping while the first one is being eaten.

Variation

Make chicken sukiyaki as above, substituting chicken for beef and using chicken fat for greasing the pan.

Beef Sukiyaki

CHRYSANTHEMUM PRAWN TEMPURA

SERVES 4

Tempura is food – mainly fish and shellfish – normally dipped in a special batter, deep-fried and served with *tempura* sauce. The oil should be at least 5-cm/2-in deep and kept at a temperature of between 150–180 C/300–350 F. The oil should be skimmed carefully during frying, otherwise little bits of batter burning in it ruin the colour and flavour. Batter is not used in the recipe which follows; *harusame* noodles made from potato or soya bean starch, available from Japanese food stores, supply the crisp outside surface.

100 g/4 oz peeled uncooked prawns
2 egg whites
pinch of salt
1 tablespoon cornflour
225 g/8 oz harusame *noodles*
oil for deep frying
6–8 chrysanthemum leaves
grated Japanese radish
grated fresh root ginger
For Tempura Sauce
300 ml/½ pint Japanese stock (page 36)
4 tablespoons Japanese soy sauce
4 tablespoons sake *(or dry sherry)*
pinch of salt

Put the prawns through a mincer then pound in a mortar to a smooth paste. Add the egg whites, salt and cornflour. Blend well and shape into strips 4–5 cm/1½–2 in long, depending on how long you like your chrysanthemum petals.

Press the prawn patties (one side only) gently but firmly into the *harusame* noodles. The idea is to preserve the round shape of the patties and at the same time to make them pick up as many 'petals' as will stick. Deep fry until lightly browned and drain on absorbent kitchen paper. Arrange the freshly cooked 'chrysanthemums' in the form of a bouquet in a large dish (a flat straw one is ideal). Decorate with washed and dried chrysanthemum leaves to complete the illusion and serve.

To make the *tempura* sauce, bring the stock, soy sauce and *sake* to the boil, season to taste and serve in a small bowl. Serve the grated radish and ginger in two small bowls.

SASHIMI

(Illustrated on page 35)

Sashimi consists of raw fish, lobster, crayfish or cuttlefish. To render it more digestible, and for added flavour, the sashimi is usually served with grated Japanese horseradish (wasabi) and invariably with Japanese soy sauce (shoyu). Garnish and presentation are of great importance in the serving of sashimi.

The Japanese are in a class by themselves when it comes to serving raw fish. As in so many other Japanese dishes, the freshest possible ingredients are used to create a landscape.

Lobsters, prawns and other crustaceans undergo a special treatment in preparation for sashimi. To ensure complete freshness, only live shellfish are used. They are killed quickly and, according to Japanese cooks, painlessly, by being stabbed with a knife in the soft part of the belly. After this, shell at once, wash the flesh with great care and continue to wash in cold running water until it stiffens. Dry on absorbent kitchen paper and the prawn or lobster is ready for use.

You can only attempt to prepare sashimi from the *freshest* of fish. If you have a good fishmonger he may well offer live shellfish. Otherwise use white fish fillets, including cod, plaice or sole, fresh mackerel, sea bream, salmon, salmon trout and squid if available. Smoked salmon or other smoked fish can also be used.

The fish must be trimmed of all bones and scales. Remove the outer skin of mackerel, leaving the distinctive markings. Cut the fish into tissue-thin slices or matchstick strips and arrange them decoratively on a platter.

For garnish use fine strips of peeled red pepper, small pieces of peeled, deseeded tomato and strips of nori. Add finely shredded carrot, cucumber and radish (use the large white radish).

To serve with the sashimi, mix about 4 tablespoons Japanese soy sauce with 2 teaspoons grated fresh root ginger to make a dip.

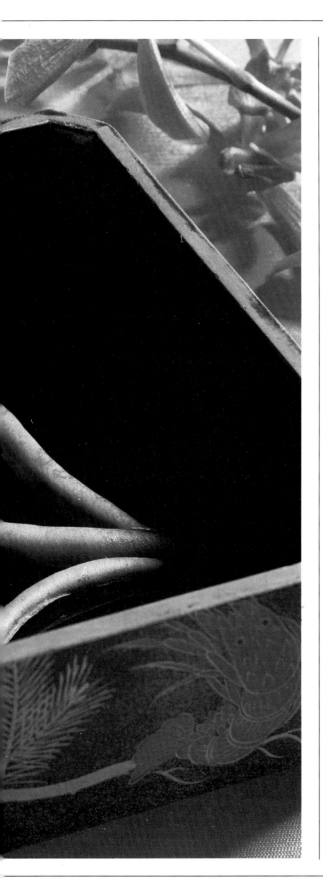

SAVOURY BLOSSOM EGG

SERVES 4

The Japanese are great observers of festivals and there are several to be celebrated every month. There are innumerable dishes of great symbolic significance which tradition prescribes for every occasion. Savoury Blossom Egg, known as *Balkatamago*, is one of the dishes in the menu laid down for the New Year Festival. Served in *jubako*, those attractive four tier lacquer boxes, this recipe is intended for the second tier of the *jubako*, which normally contains five different preparations.

4 hard-boiled eggs
few drops cochineal
$\frac{1}{4}$ teaspoon pepper
I teaspoon mixed mustard
$1\frac{1}{2}$ teaspoons Japanese soy sauce
a few cooked string beans or
French beans

Shell the eggs and mash the whites and yolks separately. Add just enough cochineal to the white of egg to tint it a delicate pink. Add the pepper, mustard and soy sauce to the yolks. Mix well, and spread the tinted egg-white on a bamboo mat (*sudare*) in an even layer. Cover with a layer of yolk. Roll up the mat, tie with string at both ends, and steam for 15 minutes. Allow to cool, unwrap and slice the two-coloured egg roll. The slices will look like flowers. Arrange two or three on each individual dish and give each flower a stem made of string bean.

Note A *sudare* is a bamboo lattice mat, available from Japanese shops.

Savoury Blossom Egg

CHICKEN BUNDLES

SERVES 6

175 g/6 oz chicken meat
1 tablespoon Japanese soy sauce
1 tablespoon sake
½ sheet nori seaweed
white of egg
oil for frying

Skin the chicken, cut into strips 5 cm/2 in long by 5 mm/¼ in thick, sprinkle with Japanese soy sauce and *sake* and leave to marinate for 1 hour.

Cut the seaweed into 1-cm/½-in strips. Taking 4–5 chicken strips at a time, make into bundles, securing round the middle with a band of seaweed dipped in white of egg to make it adhere. Fry in a very little oil, drain on a greaseproof paper and serve. Allow 3–4 small 'bundles' per portion.

GRILLED CHICKEN ON SKEWERS

SERVES 4

Pride of place among Japanese grilled dishes belongs to *yakitori* – grilled chicken on skewers.

2 tablespoons Japanese soy sauce
2 tablespoons sake
1½ tablespoons sugar
175 g/6 oz breast of chicken
100 g/4 oz chicken giblets
1 large onion
1 sweet potato
100 g/4 oz Japanese radish, grated
1 teaspoon ground ginger
freshly ground black pepper

Mix the soy sauce, *sake* and sugar to make a basting sauce and stir well. Dice the chicken and giblets, peel and slice the onion and sweet potato. Impale pieces of chicken, giblets, onion and sweet potato on long skewers.

Brush the skewered ingredients with the sauce and grill until brown on all sides, basting with the sauce from time to time.

Mix the radish with ginger, add a pinch of pepper and dip each mouthful of chicken in this mixture before eating.

STEAMED MUSHROOMS

SERVES 4

This traditional way of presenting mushrooms never fails to delight. A *dobin* is a small teapot used for cooking tree mushrooms, which are found in Japan in great abundance and are available in cans. In addition to a *dobin*, each guest also requires a small wine cup, bowl-shaped and without handles, in which the cooking liquor is served.

4 large matsutake mushrooms
1½ tablespoons sake
salt
100 g/4 oz boned breast of chicken
100 g/4 oz plaice fillet
bunch of watercress
16 gingko nuts (or chestnuts)
300 ml/½ pint Japanese stock (page 36)
1 tablespoon Japanese soy sauce
1 tablespoon lemon juice
dash of vinegar

Cut the mushrooms into small dice, sprinkle with *sake* and season with a pinch of salt. Cut the chicken and plaice into small thin slices, put together on a dish and strain the liquid from the mushrooms over them.

Shred the watercress. Heat the gingko nuts in an ungreased pan until they begin to jump, then remove their hard outer shells and boil in slightly salted water for 2 minutes or until tender. Drain.

Put the mushrooms, chicken, plaice, nuts and watercress into four *dobins* or heatproof serving dishes. Mix the stock with the soy sauce and season with ½ teaspoon salt. Divide between the *dobins* or dishes. Steam for 20 minutes.

When serving, pour the liquid from each *dobin* or dish into a wine cup provided for this purpose. Serve a small side dish of lemon juice with a dash of vinegar added to it, for dipping morsels of food before they are eaten.

TANGERINE BASKETS

SERVES 4

This is a traditional dish for the delightful Doll Festival, celebrated on the 3rd March. Little girls, in their best kimonos, gather to admire a display of both new dolls, and those which have been in the family for generations, passing from mother to daughter. The children sit on cushions on the floor, which is always covered with straw matting of unbelievable purity, equally absorbed and delight- ed with the splendour of the red-cloth-covered shelves, with tier upon tier of dolls, dolls' house furniture and accessories and the array of little dainties prepared specially for them.

4 tangerines
15 g/$\frac{1}{2}$ oz gelatine
450 ml/$\frac{3}{4}$ pint water
75 g/3 oz sugar

Cut each tangerine to make it look like a small basket with a handle on top. To do this, hold the tangerine stalk end up, make two parallel cuts 1 cm/$\frac{1}{2}$ in apart, on both sides of the top centre down one-third of the fruit. Then, cut horizontally on each side of the handle and remove the two pieces cut out. Carefully extract all the pulp and squeeze out its juice into a small bowl. You should now have a small, empty basket. Repeat the procedure for the remaining tangerines.

Dissolve the gelatine in the water in a basin over a saucepan of hot water. Add the sugar and tangerine juice, leave until the jelly begins to set, then spoon it into the tangerine baskets and chill.

Tangerine Baskets

Indonesia

The islands of Indonesia in the Malay Archipelago are a gourmet's paradise with a varied cuisine which is rich both in the fruits of the sea and tropical ingredients. The Moluccas, known as the Spice Islands, form part of this chain of islands along with Java, Sumatra and the tiny island of Bali.

Indonesian cooking is heavily influenced by Chinese culinary traditions but it makes greater use of spices, chillies and coconuts. Indonesian curries are rich, spicy and hot, cooked with coconut milk and sometimes containing fruit. Other ingredients which are used in the cooking of this part of the world include lemon grass (sereh or serai) and dried shrimps which are pounded to form blachan or blacan paste.

Indonesian meals are served with a selection of side dishes or sambals. Often the main dishes are mildly seasoned but the accompanying sambal may be quite fiery. Other side dishes may be made up of mild ingredients including tomatoes, onions and coconut with some fresh green chillies.

Rice is the staple food in most of Indonesian cooking and it forms the base for one of the most famous of Indonesian dishes, Nasi Goreng, which combines shredded pork and omelette with spicy fried rice. The following recipes will provide an insight into the full-flavoured specialities from this part of the world.

SPICED FISH

SERVES 4

(Illustrated on page 47)

450 g/1 lb mullet fillets (or other white fish)
walnut-sized piece of tamarind pod
3–4 tablespoons peanut oil
2 onions
2 cloves garlic
$\frac{1}{2}$ teaspoon fresh chilli (optional)
1 tablespoon soy sauce
2 tablespoons water
1 teaspoon soft brown sugar
juice of 1 lime or lemon

Rub the fish fillets with tamarind, then fry them in hot oil to brown both sides. Chop the onions and the garlic. Reduce the heat, add the onions and garlic to the fish and cook for 3–4 minutes. Add the chilli, if using, and fry lightly for 1 minute. Mix the soy sauce, water, sugar and lime or lemon juice and pour over the fish. Bring to the boil, simmer for 3–4 seconds and serve.

PRAWN SAMBAL

SERVES 4

All *sambals* (side dishes) are strongly flavoured with chilli, but the amount of chilli can be increased or reduced, depending on individual taste.

450 g/1 lb uncooked prawns
1 onion
1 clove garlic
2 fresh chillies, deseeded and chopped
crushed tamarind
$\frac{1}{2}$ bay leaf
2 tablespoons peanut oil
$\frac{1}{2}$ teaspoon powdered ginger
1 teaspoon sugar
300 ml/$\frac{1}{2}$ pint coconut milk (page 74)

Shell and de-vein prawns. Chop the onion and garlic, then pound with the chilli, tamarind and bay leaf in a mortar to make a smooth paste.

Heat the oil and fry the pounded ingredients in it for 3–4 minutes. Add prawns, ginger and sugar. Simmer for a few minutes, stirring constantly, then add the coconut milk; blend and simmer without boiling until the sauce thickens.

TOMATO SAMBAL

SERVES 4

(Illustrated on page 49)

3 cloves garlic
about ½ teaspoon tamarind pod
1 small onion
2–3 tablespoons peanut oil
2 fresh red chillies
450 g/1 lb tomatoes
1–2 leeks
salt
1 tablespoon brown sugar
150 ml/¼ pint coconut milk (page 74)
2 tablespoons Prawn Sambal
(opposite)

Crush the garlic and tamarind. Chop the onion. Fry the garlic, tamarind and onion in the oil for 3–4 minutes. Deseed and shred the chillies, peel and slice the tomatoes. Add the chillies and tomatoes to the pan and cook, stirring, for 2 minutes. Wash and slice the leeks, add to the pan, stir and cook for 2 minutes. Sprinkle with salt and sugar. Gradually blend in the coconut milk and prawn sambal, simmer gently for 10 minutes and serve.

Indonesian Meat and Vegetable Soup (overleaf)

SHREDDED OMELETTE

SERVES 2–4

3–4 spring onions
1 peeled tomato
100 g/4 oz cooked ham
1–2 tablespoons butter or oil
pinch each of salt and chilli powder
3–4 tablespoons soy sauce
4 eggs

Chop the spring onions. Peel and chop the tomato. Cut the ham into thin strips.

Heat the butter or oil and fry the onions until soft. Add the tomato and cook together for 2–3 minutes. Add the ham, season with salt, chilli powder and half the soy sauce. Cook for 3 minutes.

Beat the eggs and stir into the pan, cover, lower heat to minimum and cook until done. Remove the omelette, shred finely, sprinkle with the remaining soy sauce and serve.

INDONESIAN MEAT AND VEGETABLE SOUP

SERVES 8

3 onions
2 cloves garlic
I teaspoon chopped fresh root ginger
I teaspoon cumin seeds
I teaspoon coriander seeds
½ teaspoon chilli powder
I bay leaf
I dried lemon leaf or lemon grass
stalk
salt
2 tablespoons peanut oil
1.75 litres/3 pints coconut milk
(page 74)
I carrot
100 g/4 oz runner beans
175 g/6 oz cabbage or Brussels sprouts
small cauliflower
25 g/I oz lean beef
I red or green pepper
100 g/4 oz shelled peas
I teaspoon grated lemon rind
I teaspoon paprika
pinch of brown sugar
225 g/8 oz peeled cooked prawns
3–4 tablespoons grated fresh coconut
or desiccated coconut

Chop two of the onions, the garlic and ginger and blend in a liquidiser or pound in a mortar with the cumin and coriander seeds, chilli powder, bay leaf, lemon leaf and a teaspoon of salt until all these ingredients are reduced to a smooth paste. In a large saucepan cook the paste for 3 minutes in I tablespoon of the oil, stirring constantly. Dilute with coconut milk, blend and bring to the boil.

Shred the carrot, beans and cabbage or Brussels sprouts. Divide the cauliflower into florets. Mince the beef, deseed and shred the pepper. Add the carrot, beans, cabbage, peas, cauliflower, beef, lemon rind and pepper to the pan. Season with salt and paprika, sprinkle with sugar. Cook over a low heat for 15–20 minutes and make sure you have enough coconut milk to prevent the soup from drying out.

Slice the third onion finely and fry in the remaining oil until very crisp. Transfer to a serving bowl, garnish with the prawns, fried onion and grated coconut and serve.

BEEF SATAY

SERVES 4

Satay is popular over a vast area, from Java to Hong Kong; it is served at elegant cocktail parties (cooked on small bamboo skewers, it can easily be handed around), popular restaurants and even on street corners – rather like hot dogs or roasted chestnuts are sold in the West.

I tablespoon blanched almonds
I slice fresh root ginger
I teaspoon coriander seeds
I teaspoon turmeric
300 ml/½ pint coconut milk (page 74)
450 g/I lb lean frying steak (rump,
fillet or sirloin)
salt and freshly ground black pepper
I teaspoon brown sugar

Pound the almonds, ginger, coriander seeds, and turmeric to a paste, then gradually dilute with the coconut milk. Cut the beef into bite-sized cubes, season to taste with salt and pepper, put into the spiced coconut milk and leave to marinate for 2 hours.

Drain the beef, thread on skewers, sprinkle with sugar and grill, turning and basting frequently with the coconut marinade. Serve with Satay Sauce (page 49).

BRAISED PORK

SERVES 4

450 g/I lb lean pork
2 tablespoons peanut oil
I clove garlic
I onion
75 ml/3 fl oz soy sauce
2 tablespoons water
I teaspoon lemon juice
I teaspoon brown sugar

Cut the pork into bite-sized cubes. Heat the oil in a saucepan, add and brown the pork. Finely chop the garlic and onion and add to the pork. Fry together for 3 minutes.

Blend the soy sauce with the water, lemon juice and sugar, pour the mixture over the pork and simmer uncovered for 12–15 minutes. Serve hot.

FRITTERS

SERVES 4

Known as *kemangi* these are probably Dutch. This is one of the classic side dishes for banquets and several kinds of *kemangi* can be served at a *rijstafel* meal (banquet).

225 g/8 oz cooked meat or chicken
600 ml/1 pint white sauce (opposite)
salt and pepper
juice of $\frac{1}{2}$ lime
$1\frac{1}{2}$ teaspoons chopped parsley
peanut oil for deep frying
flour for coating
1–2 eggs, beaten
100 g/4 oz dry breadcrumbs
Satay Sauce (page 49)

Mince the meat. Prepare the white sauce. When it thickens, check the seasoning and stir in the lime juice. Remove from heat, add the meat and parsley, mix well and spread the mixture on a shallow dish to cool. Heat the oil for deep frying.

Taking a teaspoon of the mixture at a time, shape into little balls, roll in flour, dip in beaten egg, coat with breadcrumbs and deep fry, until golden. Drain on absorbent kitchen paper and serve with satay sauce in a separate sauce boat. The above amount should make 20–25 fritters.

WHITE SAUCE

MAKES ABOUT 600ML / 1 PINT

50 g/2 oz butter
50 g/2 oz plain flour
600 ml/1 pint milk or stock
salt and pepper

Melt the butter over a low heat, stir in the flour and cook gently for 3 minutes, stirring all the time. Remove from the heat, blend in half the liquid, return to the heat and cook, stirring vigorously. When the sauce thickens, add the rest of the liquid. Simmer until thickened to the desired consistency. Season to taste.

Spiced Fish (page 44)

INDONESIAN FRIED RICE

SERVES 4

This *Nasi Goreng* is probably the best-known Indonesian rice dish. It is ample and delicious. Nasi means rice and goreng means fried.

225 g/8 oz long-grain rice
450 ml/¾ pint water
50 g/2 oz dried shrimps
2 onions
1 clove garlic
175 g/6 oz peanut oil
1 fresh chilli or ½ teaspoon chilli powder
225 g/8 oz cooked meat or chicken or fish
salt and pepper
3 eggs for omelette
thinly sliced cucumber to garnish

Wash the rice and cook in the water for 10 minutes. Drain thoroughly, spread on a large dish and leave to cool. Soak the dried shrimps (available from Chinese food shops) in enough water to cover. Chop the onions and garlic finely.

Heat the oil in a large frying pan or a Chinese wok. Fry the onions until they turn transparent. Add the garlic and fry for 1 minute. Shred the chilli, add to the pan, fry for 3 minutes. Shred the meat, chicken or fish, add to the pan and fry for 2 minutes, stirring all the time. Add the rice. Drain the shrimps and add to the pan. Fry on a fairly high flame, stirring frequently, until the rice turns a pale golden colour. Season to taste. Put on a heated serving dish and keep hot. Make a shredded omelette (page 45) seasoning the eggs only with salt and pepper. Arrange the shredded omelette on top of the rice, garnish with cucumber slices and serve piping hot.

MIXED VEGETABLE PICKLE

SERVES 6–8

Atjar – mixed vegetable pickle – is a condiment for every meal. It is an essential side dish for a banquet and it is also served as an accompaniment to *nasi goreng*. No self-respecting Indonesian housewife would ever serve pickles bought from a shop and no bottled produce could compete with fresh home-made *atjar*. Here is a simple recipe and the ingredients to be pickled can be varied according to season and taste.

2 green peppers
1 carrot
½ cucumber
100 g/4 oz runner beans
225 g/8 oz shallots
salt
4–5 blanched almonds
1 teaspoon turmeric
2 cloves garlic
2.5-cm/1-in slice fresh root ginger
600 ml/1 pint vinegar
150 ml/¼ pint water
1–1½ tablespoons brown sugar

Deseed the peppers and shred. Slice the carrot, cucumber and beans. Peel the shallots. Drop the peppers, carrot, cucumber, beans and shallots into enough salted boiling water to cover, cook for 4–5 minutes and drain well.

Pound the almonds, turmeric, garlic and ginger in a mortar, or blend them in a liquidiser to reduce them to a smooth paste. Gradually dilute with the vinegar and water. Season with salt to taste. Add the sugar, mix well and bring to the boil in a saucepan. Add the par-boiled vegetables and cook for 10 minutes. Allow to cool, then chill. Serve cold.

SATAY SAUCE

SERVES 4

The popular use of peanuts to make a sauce is a distinctive feature of Indonesian cooking.

2 onions
1–2 tablespoons peanut oil
75 g/3 oz roasted peanuts
½ teaspoon chilli powder
150 ml/¼ pint warm water
1 teaspoon brown sugar
salt
1 tablespoon soy sauce
juice of ½ lime or lemon

Slice one onion and fry in hot oil. Chop the second onion finely, put in a mortar with the peanuts and chilli powder and pound to a paste or blend in a liquidiser. Add the paste to the fried onion and fry together for 3 minutes, stirring well. Gradually dilute with the water and stir in the sugar. Cook for a few minutes to concentrate the sauce to the consistency of single cream. Season with salt to taste, add the soy sauce and lime or lemon juice, stir and use for basting or serving with all *satay* dishes.

Tomato Sambal (page 45)

CRISPY BANANAS

SERVES 4

These crispy bananas – *pisang goreng* – add interest in terms of texture to the meal. The fruit also has a cooling effect which complements the fiery heat of the *sambals*.

peanut oil for deep frying
4 ripe bananas
juice of ½ lemon
2–3 tablespoons brown sugar

Heat the oil. Peel and cut the bananas in half lengthways, dip in the lemon juice, coat with brown sugar and fry until crisp and golden. Drain on absorbent kitchen paper and serve at once.

Thailand

In Thailand a meal might well open with soup to be followed by an assortment of main dishes, one or two side dishes and large quantities of rice. Alternatively, the rice may even be served as the central dish.

Many of the dishes are very hot, or mildly spiced and served with fiery accompaniments. The meal may well be served khan toke *style on a low, round, brass table at which the diners sit cross-legged on cushions. Traditionally the* khan toke *meal consists of five different dishes served with rice.*

The ingredients which give Thai cooking its distinctive style include seafoods, beef and poultry cooked with fragrant lemons and limes, large quantities of hot chillies, coconut milk, lemon grass, peanuts, papaya and mango. Nampla, *a pungent fish sauce, is used extensively as a flavouring. Coriander is another well-favoured flavouring ingredient. Fresh vegetables and eggs are also used, as are noodles.*

Desserts and cakes are prepared in addition to the savoury foods but some of these sweet specialities require expert knowledge for their successful preparation. One simple recipe for Caramelized Bananas is included at the end of the chapter.

THAI-STYLE CHICKEN AND MUSHROOM SOUP

SERVES 4

The Thais have many interesting soups. They like to combine pork and shellfish, chicken and prawns or lobster, flavoured with unbiquitous *nam pla* (page 75).

1 chicken
1 onion
2 litres/3½ pints water
175 g/6 oz button mushrooms
2–3 cloves garlic
1 teaspoon ground coriander
½ teaspoon dried red chillies
2 tablespoons chicken fat
2 teaspoons nam pla *or 1 tablespoon anchovy paste mixed with*
1 tablespoon soy sauce
salt
1 tablespoon palm sugar
1 teaspoon soy sauce
1 tablespoon chopped parsley

Cook the chicken and its giblets with the onion in the water until tender. Remove, take the flesh off the bones and slice the chicken meat and the giblets. Drop the bones back into the stock. Continue to simmer the stock for at least an hour to reduce and concentrate it, then strain.

Bring the mushrooms to the boil in enough water to cover, cook for 2 minutes and drain. Pound the garlic, coriander and chillies into a paste. Heat the chicken fat and fry the paste and *nam pla* or anchovy paste in it for 3 minutes, stirring all the time.

Add the chicken and cook, stirring, for 2 minutes. Season with salt to taste, sprinkle with the sugar, pour in the stock. Bring to the boil, add the mushrooms and soy sauce, cover and simmer for 5 minutes, then sprinkle with chopped parsley and serve.

Variation

Chicken, Prawn and Cucumber Soup Follow instructions for Chicken and Mushroom soup, but omit the mushrooms and add 225 g/8 oz peeled cooked prawns and 175 g/6 oz diced peeled cucumber.

FISH WITH MUSHROOMS AND SWEET AND SOUR SAUCE

SERVES 6

Sweet and sour dishes are very popular in Thailand. Fish and shellfish, beef and pork, chicken and pigeons, are cooked in sweet and sour sauce.

6 sole fillets
1 tablespoon lime or lemon juice
75 g/3 oz cornflour
salt
3 tablespoons light ale or lager
4 tablespoons peanut oil
25 g/1 oz spring onions
1 tablespoon preserved stem ginger
2 tablespoons sugar
pinch of ground ginger
4–5 tablespoons vinegar
$\frac{1}{2}$ tablespoon soy sauce
100 g/4 oz fresh mushrooms
3 tablespoons cold water

Thai-style Chicken and Mushroom Soup (opposite)

Cut the fillets into diagonal slices, sprinkle with lime or lemon juice and leave for a few minutes, while you make the batter.

Season 65 g/$2\frac{1}{2}$ oz of the cornflour with a generous pinch of salt and blend in the beer. Blend in half a tablespoon of the oil and stir well. Coat the fillets with this batter. Heat the remaining oil and fry the fish until brown on all sides. Remove from pan, drain on absorbent kitchen paper to get rid of excess oil, and keep hot on a serving dish.

Chop the spring onions and preserved ginger. Combine the spring onions with the sugar and chopped and ground ginger; add the vinegar and soy sauce, put over a low heat and stir well to dissolve the sugar. Slice the mushrooms, add to the pan and simmer for 5–6 minutes.

Blend the remaining cornflour with the water, stir into the sauce and continue to simmer until the sauce thickens, then pour over the fish and serve.

LOBSTER SALAD

SERVES 4

Salad is a misleading term in Thai cookery. The Thai word is *yum* and a *yum* is a must on a Thai menu. All kinds of raw shredded vegetables, fruit, leaves, vine shoots, grasses, often mixed with dried shrimps, dressed with soy sauce or a mixture of *nam pla* and lime juice and garnished with chopped chillies, are served as salads.

2 small cooked lobsters
2 green peppers
1 clove garlic
3–4 shallots
1–2 tablespoons peanut oil
1–2 peaches
2 tablespoons peanuts
1 tablespoon soy sauce
150 ml/¼ pint coconut milk (page 74)

Cut the lobsters in half lengthways, remove the meat and cut into bite-sized pieces. Arrange on a serving dish. Cut the peppers in half, remove seeds, rinse, drop into boiling water for one minute, drain and cut into shreds. Chop the garlic and shallots, heat the oil and fry garlic and shallots until transparent.

Allow to cool. Spread the mixture over the lobster. Dip the peaches into boiling water for a few seconds and slip off the skin. Slice the peaches. Chop the peanuts. Add the peach slices, chopped peanuts, soy sauce, and coconut milk to the salad. Stir, sprinkle with shredded green pepper, and serve cold.

Variation

Prawn Salad As above, but using 450 g/1 lb prawns instead of lobster. Cook prawns for 7–8 minutes. Substitute peeled sliced pears or grated apples for peaches.

Lobster Salad

THAI-STYLE CRAB

SERVES 4

There are many variations of Crab, Thai style, *poo cha*. Celery seeds and thyme can be substituted for basil and coriander. The one vital ingredient is *nam pla* (page 75).

Instead of baking the crab meat, it can be packed into shells, brushed with beaten egg and deep fried in hot fat for 5 minutes or until nicely brown.

4 dressed crabs
100 g/4 oz bean shoots
6 spring onions
1 clove garlic
pinch of sweet basil
$\frac{3}{4}$ teaspoon coriander seeds
1 egg
3 tablespoons coconut milk (page 74)
salt and pepper
1 tablespoon plain flour
1 tablespoon nam pla or 1 tablespoon anchovy paste with 1 tablespoon soy sauce

Put all the crab meat in a saucepan. Wash and dry the shells and put to one side. Wash the bean shoots, trim off roots, drain well, and add to the crab meat. Finely chop the spring onions, garlic, basil and coriander seeds and mix with the crab meat and bean shoots. Heat gently and cook for 1–2 minutes without any fat. Remove from heat.

Beat the egg, blend in the coconut milk, season to taste with salt and freshly ground black pepper. Heat over a pan of simmering water, sprinkle in the flour, a little at a time, blending it in well. Flavour with *nam pla* or anchovy paste blended with soy sauce. Mix well. Simmer gently, stirring, until the sauce is smooth and thick. Mix the sauce with the crab mixture, season to taste and spoon into the crab shells. Bake in a moderately hot oven (190C, 375F, gas 5) for 20–25 minutes.

THAI-STYLE BEEF

SERVES 6

This can be described as strips of beef cooked in coconut milk, served on a bed of lightly cooked spinach, dressed with coconut cream, and served with rice. The amount of chillies can be increased if you want the sauce really hot.

675 g/ 1$\frac{1}{2}$ lb lean rump steak
900 ml/ 1$\frac{1}{2}$ pints coconut milk (page 74)
1$\frac{1}{2}$ tablespoons soy sauce
1 tablespoon brown sugar
20 g/$\frac{3}{4}$ oz roasted peanuts, ground
675 g/ 1$\frac{1}{2}$ lb spinach
salt
6 spring onions
2 cloves garlic
2–3 slices fresh root ginger
2–3 dried red chillies
1 teaspoon cornflour
2 tablespoons cold water
300 ml/$\frac{1}{2}$ pint coconut cream (page 74)

Cut the beef into thin strips, put in a pan, cover with the coconut milk, reserving 175 ml/6 fl oz for later use. Gently bring to the boil, simmer for 5 minutes. Add the soy sauce, sugar and peanuts.

Wash the spinach, cook for 2–3 minutes, just covering the leaves with water. Drain, season with salt and keep hot. Chop the spring onions, garlic, ginger and chillies then pound with a pinch of salt, gradually adding the reserved coconut milk. Blend well and stir the mixture into the pan. Simmer for 2–3 minutes. Dilute the cornflour with the water and stir into the pan. Simmer, stirring until the sauce thickens. Check seasoning. Have the spinach ready on a heated serving dish. Spoon the beef and the sauce over it. Top with the coconut cream and serve.

Variations

Thai-style Veal As above, using veal instead of beef.
Thai-style Chicken As above, using chicken instead of beef.

THAI NOODLES

SERVES 4–6

450 g/1 lb Chinese rice noodles
1 medium onion
3–4 cloves garlic
175 g/6 oz lean pork
225 g/8 oz chicken meat
100 g/4 oz crab meat
225 g/8 oz uncooked prawns
1 square bean curd
100–175 g/4–6 oz bean sprouts
300 ml/½ pint oil for frying
1 tablespoon soy sauce
1 tablespoon vinegar
1 tablespoon nam pla or
anchovy paste
1 tablespoon sugar
salt
3–4 spring onions
4 eggs
pinch of ground coriander
red chillies (optional)

Break the noodles into pieces and drop into boiling salted water. Simmer for 1 minute, drain well and spread on a dish. Leave to dry out for 30 minutes.

Chop the onion and garlic. Slice the pork and chicken meat. Flake the crab meat. Peel, de-vein and chop the prawns. Cut the bean curd into small dice. Pick over, wash and drain the bean sprouts.

Heat 250 ml/8 fl oz of the oil in a deep frying pan and fry the noodles until crisp and pale golden, turning twice. Remove, drain thoroughly and put aside.

Heat the remaining oil in a frying pan and lightly fry the onion and garlic. Add the pork and cook for 8–10 minutes, stirring frequently. Add the chicken and cook, stirring, for 3 minutes. Add the crab meat, prawns and bean curd, cook, stirring, for a few minutes until the chicken and prawns change colour. Season with the soy sauce, vinegar, *nam pla*, sugar and salt to taste. Mix well, simmer on low heat for 5 minutes. Chop the spring onions. Beat the eggs and pour into the pan, stir to mix. As soon as the egg begins to set, add the bean sprouts and noodles and cook, stirring, for a couple of minutes to heat through. Transfer to a heated serving dish, sprinkle with spring onions and the coriander, garnish with red chillies, if liked, and serve.

CARAMELISED BANANA SLICES

SERVES 4

Thai cooks make delightful desserts. Here is a popular recipe for bananas, which can be applied with equal success to apples, pears, oranges, tangerines, pineapple, or to mixed fruit slices which can be served plain, with coconut cream or with whipped cream.

Provide each guest with a bowl of iced water for dipping banana slices before eating.

4 ripe firm bananas
lime or lemon juice
peanut oil for deep frying
6 tablespoons sugar
3 tablespoons water

Peel the bananas, slice thinly lengthways, sprinkle with lime or lemon juice and leave while you heat the oil and prepare the caramel.

To make the syrup, slowly melt the sugar in water over a low heat, then increase heat and let the mixture boil until it turns a pale caramel colour — do not allow it to brown. To arrest excessive cooking, as soon as the syrup turns pale golden, remove the pan from the heat and stand it on a tea-towel, dipped in cold water and wrung out.

Deep-fry the banana slices, a few at a time, for a few seconds. Remove with a slotted spoon to a heated metal dish. Continue in this manner until all the slices are fried and laid out on the serving dish, which should be big enough to take them in a single layer.

Reheat the syrup and pour it over the banana slices in an even trickle so that it coats all the slices. Serve at once.

Caramelised Banana Slices

Malaysia

Malaysian food is influenced by the characteristics of both Indian and Chinese cooking as you will see from the limited selection of dishes which is included in this chapter.

The curries cooked here are fiery hot (unlike many of their Indian counterparts) as well as creamy with the addition of coconut milk. Spiced up with garlic, lemon grass, turmeric, coriander and tamarind, if the finished dish is slightly mild, then the chances are that it will be accompanied by a tiny dish of raw, sliced chillies, just to add extra heat to the meal!

Seafoods are plentiful and strongly flavoured dried shrimp paste is used extensively. Peanuts are also used to flavour and thicken certain dishes. For example, satay dishes are popular here as in other oriental cookery. Chinese cabbage, beansprouts and okra are just some of the vegetables which may be cooked in stir-fries. Beancurd – either the soft variety or a firmer type – is used in stir-fries and noodles are popular. These may be egg noodles or flat, white, rice noodles.

Of course, as in all countries of the Orient rice is an important food. Served plain boiled, spiced up in pilaus or fried Chinese style, the various methods of preparing and serving this simple, staple ingredient reflects the interesting and diverse styles which are to be found in Malaysian cooking.

CHICKEN SOUP

SERVES 6–8

Malaysian soups, which are not necessarily served at the start of the meal, are based on meat, poultry, fish or vegetable stocks, prepared in the usual way. However, there is no such thing as a stock pot permanently on the simmer and refrigerators are not easy to come by, particularly in the country, so stock has to be made fresh. To hasten the cooking process, all ingredients are cut into small pieces. This recipe does not require any stock.

1 chicken, jointed
2 litres/3½ pints water
1 tablespoon salt
2 medium onions
1 teaspoon fresh root ginger
1 tablespoon soy sauce
3 tablespoons peanut oil
175 g/6 oz long-grain rice
pinch of chilli powder
2–3 hard-boiled eggs to garnish

Put the chicken in a pan with water and salt, bring to the boil and skim until no more scum rises to the surface. Quarter 1 of the onions and add to the pan with the ginger. Simmer for 1–1½ hours, or until the chicken is tender. Strain the stock. Bone the chicken, shred the meat, and sprinkle with the soy sauce. Cut the remaining onion into thin slices. Fry in half the oil, until pale golden. Remove, drain well and keep hot. Add the remaining oil, and gently fry the rice until transparent, stirring all the time.

Bring the stock to the boil. Add the rice and chilli powder. Simmer gently for 18–20 minutes, by which time the rice should be tender. Add the chicken, check seasoning, adding more salt and chilli if needed. Re-heat and serve with a topping of fried onions and slices of hard-boiled egg.

PRAWN CRACKERS

(Illustrated on page 59)

These prawn crackers or shrimp slices are popular at cocktail parties and make an interesting change from crisps. Like many other good things, these originally come from China. They are used in oriental cookery the way croûtons are used in French classical dishes. Excellent sprinkled over soups or dishes with lots of gravy.

peanut oil for deep frying
1 packet prawn crackers

Heat the oil for deep frying and drop into it a few crackers at a time. As soon as they open up and float up to the surface – which takes only a few seconds – take them out with a slotted spoon and drain well. Continue until all are done.

The prawn crackers will become much larger in size. On no account should they be allowed to brown, therefore care should be taken not to over-heat the oil. If the crackers tend to turn even pale brown, reduce the heat.

Serve as you would _croûtons_, allowing your guests to help themselves at table. Enough prawn crackers for four people can be prepared in 5 minutes.

Chicken Soup (opposite)

PRAWNS IN COCONUT

SERVES 4

2 large onions, chopped
2–3 tablespoons ghee
1 teaspoon garam masala (page 74)
2 dried red chillies
1 green pepper
450 g/1 lb peeled cooked prawns
salt
300 ml/½ pint coconut milk (page 74)

Brown the onions lightly in ghee, stir in the garam masala and cook, stirring, for 3 minutes.

Deseed and chop the chillies. Deseed and slice the green pepper. Add the chilli and green pepper to the onion, cover and simmer over a low heat for 10 minutes. Add the prawns, season and mix well. Cook for 1 minute. Reduce heat, add the coconut milk. Heat through. _Do not boil._ Serve with rice.

MALAY FISH CASSEROLE

SERVES 4

To be authentic, this dish really requires certain varieties of fish which are not available in Europe, known by their Malay names as *ikan merah*, *tenggiri*, or *kurau*. But cooks everywhere else have learned to make creditable versions by using substitutes. All good quality white fish is suitable.

675 g/ 1½ lb white fish fillet
3 tablespoons ghee or oil
1 red chilli
1 tablespoon chopped fresh root ginger
225 g/8 oz shallots
1 teaspoon turmeric
salt
300 ml/½ pint thick coconut cream (page 74)
300 ml/½ pint coconut milk (page 74)
Garnish
crisp fried onion rings
red and green chillies

Cut the fish into portions, wipe and brown lightly in 1–2 tablespoons of the *ghee*. Remove from pan.

Deseed the chilli, shred the ginger and slice the shallots. Add the remaining *ghee* to the pan and fry the chilli, ginger and shallots, stirring, for 3–4 minutes. Sprinkle in the turmeric, add salt, lower heat and carefully blend in half the coconut cream and all the milk.

Add the fish, simmer on lowest possible heat for 8–10 minutes, testing the fish for readiness from time to time. Add the remaining coconut cream, check seasoning and re-heat. Garnish with onion rings, decorate with red and green chillies and serve with rice.

FISH COOKED IN BANANA LEAVES

SERVES 6

3 tablespoons butter
50 g/2 oz fresh coconut, grated
2 medium onions
1–2 cloves garlic
2 dried red chillies or ¼ teaspoon chilli powder
pinch of turmeric
150 ml/¼ pint coconut milk (page 74)
20 peeled cooked prawns
675 g/ 1½ lb white fish fillet
2–3 tablespoons ground cashew nuts
2 eggs
salt
3 banana leaves
1–2 tablespoons oil

Heat half the butter and lightly fry the coconut, stirring constantly, until it turns uniformly pale golden. Remove from pan.

Chop the onions and garlic, and brown lightly in the remaining butter. Pound the coconut, onion, garlic, chillies and turmeric or blend in a liquidiser to reduce to a paste. Heat gently. Remove from heat. Gradually dilute with coconut milk, transfer to a double boiler and simmer the sauce for 10–15 minutes, or until it thickens. Remove from heat and allow to cool.

Chop the prawns and fish or put through a mincer. Put in a mixing bowl, and add the cashew nuts and the coconut sauce. Blend in the eggs, season to taste and mix well. Cut the banana leaves (or whatever you are using for wrapping) into six 20-cm/8-in squares and brush them lightly with the oil. Divide the mixture equally between them and neatly fold in the edges to form long narrow envelopes, enclosing the filling securely. Pin each with a cocktail stick to prevent the package unwrapping. This will not be necessary if you are using foil or paper. Either steam or bake in a lightly greased pan in a moderately hot oven (190 C, 375 F, gas 5) for 35–40 minutes.

Discard the cocktail sticks and serve *otak otak* piping hot in the leaves, or remove from foil or paper before serving.

FISH CURRY

SERVES 4

Malayan housewives take great care in preparing fish curries. There are many kinds of fish in Malaya advocated for curries, including shad, mackerel, halibut, pomfret, sea bass, garoupa, but all white fish is suitable. It is the tamarind juice which gives Malay curries their distinctive sour flavour. If tamarind is not available, use lemon juice.

450 g/1 lb halibut
salt and pepper
2 large onions
2–3 dried chillies
pinch of ground coriander
pinch of ground cumin
1 clove garlic
3 tablespoons tamarind juice (see below) or 4 tablespoons lemon juice
$\frac{1}{4}$ teaspoon turmeric
2 tablespoons oil
$1\frac{1}{2}$ tablespoons blachan
300 ml/$\frac{1}{2}$ pint thick coconut milk (page 74)

Fillet the halibut, cut into uniform small pieces and season with salt and pepper. Chop the onions, then pound with the chillies, coriander, cumin, garlic and tamarind in a mortar or blend in a liquidiser to reduce to a paste. Add the turmeric, blend well, then fry the mixture in hot oil for 2 minutes, stirring briskly. Add *blachan*, blend it in, cook for 1 minute. Add the fish and coconut milk, simmer gently for 7–8 minutes. Serve with plain boiled rice.

Tamarind Juice Tamarind pods have seeds encased in a brown, tart pulp. The pods are peeled and the pulp is soaked in water, to separate pulp from seeds, then squeezed and strained. The resulting juice, called *asam* in Malaya, is ready to be used for fish curries. For 2 tablespoons of tamarind pulp allow 6 tablespoons water. Dishes prepared with tamarind juice should be eaten the same day. Tamarind pods can be bought in shops specialising in oriental produce.

Prawn Crackers (page 57)

CURRIED EGGS IN COCONUT SAUCE

SERVES 4

In Malaysia, where Chinese, Malay and Indian schools of cooking traditions meet, there are many small eating places which cater for clients who observe various religious taboos. This recipe is safe for the Indian who is not strictly vegetarian, for a Chinese buddhist, and for anyone who likes his eggs hot. The original recipe uses three times the amount of chillies given here!

Served with rice, with a salad and fruit to follow, this curry – *Telor Masak Lemak* – makes a delicious light lunch.

4 eggs
2 small onions
1–2 cloves garlic
2–3 red chillies
2.5-cm/1-in piece fresh root ginger
2 tablespoons coconut oil
2 sprigs curry leaves or 1 tablespoon
garam masala (page 74)
1½ teaspoons ground turmeric
300 ml/½ pint coconut milk (page 74)
5 tablespoons tamarind juice
(pages 59 and 75)
150 ml/¼ pint coconut cream (page 74)

Hard-boil the eggs, plunge into cold water, shell and leave in a bowl of warm water.

Slice the onions and garlic finely. Wash the chillies, cut in half lengthways and remove seeds. Peel and slice the ginger.

Heat the oil and fry the onion, garlic, chillies and ginger with the curry leaves for 3 minutes, stirring all the time. Add the turmeric and fry for another minute, blending the ingredients. Reduce heat. Little by little add the coconut milk, simmer for a few seconds, then add the tamarind juice. Keep the sauce at lowest possible simmering heat to prevent curdling. Put in the whole shelled eggs, spoon the sauce over them and heat them through. Just before serving, add the coconut cream, heat through gently without allowing the sauce to come to the boil and serve at once.

CHICKEN WITH GREEN PEPPERS

SERVES 4–6

There is a fascinating 'street' in Singapore which, strictly speaking, is no more than a stretch of wasteland, but it leads a marvellous double life. During the day it is a dull and sedate car park. At night it is an enormous eating fair, packed with stalls and mobile kitchens, each offering a distinctive speciality. Most of the cooks are Chinese and it is rumoured that the expensive cars occupying the car park during the day belong to them. There are, however, Malay dishes to be had as well, such as this one.

1 chicken
1 large onion
2 cloves garlic
3 tablespoons butter
knob of fresh root ginger
salt
juice of 1 lime
150 ml/¼ pint water
½ teaspoon turmeric
4–5 green peppers

Joint the chicken. Chop the onion and garlic finely and, in a flameproof casserole, fry in hot butter until soft. Add the chicken joints and brown lightly on all sides. Pound the ginger. Sprinkle the chicken with salt and ginger, cover and cook over a low heat for 20–30 minutes, turning chicken once. Dilute the lime juice with water and add the mixture to the casserole. Stir in the turmeric.

Deseed and dice the peppers, add to the chicken and continue to simmer for 10–15 minutes until the chicken is tender.

Serve with plain boiled rice.

MALAY STUFFED CABBAGE

SERVES 6

Stuffed cabbage leaves are served in many parts of Europe and the Orient. The distinguishing feature of the Malaysian variety is the filling.

*1 medium white cabbage
boiling water
salt
4 shallots
3–4 spring onions
175 g/6 oz uncooked chicken meat
175 g/6 oz peeled uncooked prawns
2 tablespoons soy sauce
freshly ground pepper
3 tablespoons oil
175 ml/6 fl oz chicken stock
1 tablespoon fresh lime or lemon
juice*

Remove and discard the outer leaves of the cabbage. Wash the cabbage, then put it into boiling salted water, bring back to the boil and simmer for 2 minutes, remove, drain and put on a cloth. Taking care not to scald your fingers, carefully detach the leaves. Trim off the thick veins and edges to give the leaves a more or less uniform thickness.

Trim the shallots and spring onions. Mince together the shallots, onions, chicken and prawns. Season with half the soy sauce and pepper to taste. Mix the filling well and put a small portion on each cabbage leaf, fold in the sides and roll up the leaves.

Heat the oil in a large saucepan. Add the cabbage rolls and fry to brown on all sides. Add the stock and remaining soy sauce, cover and simmer for 20 minutes. Remove the stuffed cabbage leaves with a slotted spoon and transfer to a heated serving dish. Allow to cool. Just before serving, sprinkle with the lime juice.

Curried Eggs in Coconut Sauce (opposite)

CABBAGE AND BEAN SALAD

SERVES 6

This dish – *gado-gado* – originates from Indonesia where it is served as a delightful salad of cucumbers, bean sprouts and red chillies, dressed with peanut sauce. Singapore, being the sort of melting pot it is, has 'naturalised' *gado-gado* which is featured prominently on Malaysian menus. The Chinese prawn crackers give it a pleasant extra crunchiness. They should be fried in advance and left to cool.

$\frac{1}{2}$ *Chinese cabbage or small white cabbage*
225 g/8 oz French beans
salt
1 crisp lettuce
6 potatoes, boiled
2–3 hard-boiled eggs
For gado-gado sauce
6 shallots
2 cloves garlic
1 tablespoon peanut oil
2 slices fresh root ginger
1$\frac{1}{2}$ tablespoons peanut butter
4–5 tablespoons warm water
chilli powder
crisp fried prawn crackers (page 56)

In separate pans lightly boil the cabbage and beans in salted water for 4–6 minutes. They should remain crisp, so do not overcook. Drain well and slice.

Wash the lettuce, shake off water and arrange lettuce in a salad dish.

Slice the potatoes and eggs.

Slice the shallots and chop the garlic. Fry in hot peanut oil until golden. Chop the ginger and with the peanut butter add to the shallots and garlic. Add enough water to make a thick gravy. Season with salt and chilli powder to taste, then simmer, stirring, for 5 minutes. Keep the sauce hot while you complete the salad. Arrange the cabbage, beans, potatoes and egg slices in layers in the lettuce-lined dish. Pour the hot sauce over the salad, sprinkle with prawn crackers and serve at once.

SAGO WITH COCONUT CREAM AND PALM SUGAR

SERVES 6

This is a very famous dessert of Indonesian origin, but widely popular throughout Malaysia. It is a good example of the way Indonesian culinary genius has managed to turn sago into an exquisite sweet. It gets its special flavour from the two sauces served with it: a coconut cream one and a palm sugar syrup. Whenever possible, palm sugar (called *gula malacca*) should be used. Soft dark brown sugar can be used as an alternative.

600 ml/1 pint water
225 g/8 oz sago
300 ml/$\frac{1}{2}$ pint thick coconut milk (page 74)
pinch of salt
100 g/4 oz palm sugar

Bring the water to the boil, add the sago and cook, stirring, until the mixture thickens to a paste. Remove from heat and decant into a rinsed mould or into individual serving dishes. Leave to cool.

Now make the two sauces.

First, gently heat the coconut milk, which should be creamy. Season with a little salt and simmer until it thickens. Remove from heat, pour into a serving jug and leave to cool.

For the second sauce, cut up the palm sugar and put in a pan with 150 ml/$\frac{1}{4}$ pint boiling water. Simmer the syrup, stirring, until it thickens slightly. Remove from heat and allow to cool.

Turn the sago out of the mould as you would any jelly, or serve in individual dessert dishes. Pour some of each sauce over the pudding and serve.

Sago with Coconut Cream and Palm Sugar

India

The recipes in this chapter represent a cuisine which, sadly, is often mistakenly dismissed as hot, spicy and oily. Here you will find that Indian dishes are often carefully prepared and flavoured with sweet, mild spices, then enriched by the addition of nuts and yogurt. There are many regional variations within Indian cuisine, so it is not correct to completely dismiss the hotter dishes, for they too play an important part on any menu.

Fish, poultry, beef and lamb are the common ingredients used in main dishes. (Pork is not eaten by the majority of the population.) However, many Indians follow a vegetarian diet and this is reflected in the wide variety of delicious, spiced vegetable dishes, lentils and other pulses, spicy pilaus and vegetarian snacks, which are cooked in India.

Indian breads are served as well as or instead of rice. These may be leavened and baked (usually in a tandoor: a clay oven) and are ideal for mopping up the juices of the main dish. Deep fried, puffed breads are light and crisp, or there are some which are cooked on a griddle to make satisfying, flat pancake-type breads.

Yogurt-based side dishes and chutneys are served with an Indian meal. Sweetmeats are also served between courses or to be eaten alternately with savoury foods instead rather than being presented as a separate course at the end of the meal.

MULLIGATAWNY

SERVES 4

In its anglicised version, mulligatawny is considered an English speciality and is to be found in most English cookery books. It is a far cry from the original Southern Indian product. The name means 'pepper-water' and it can be mouth scorching. The soup can be made with meat, chicken, fish or vegetable stock. There is also a plain pepper water made of spices, fried in *ghee*, and water acidulated with tamarind juice. In India pepper water is often served with dry curry dishes.

> 175 g/6 oz red lentils (dhal)
> 2 onions
> 1 bay leaf
> 600 ml/1 pint water
> 1 clove garlic
> 1½ tablespoons ghee
> 1 tablespoon garam masala (page 74)
> 1.4 litres/2½ pints chicken stock
> salt
> 4–5 tablespoons coconut cream (page 74)
> 1 lemon

Pick over the lentils, wash, put in a bowl, cover with cold water and leave to soak for 1½–2 hours.

Slice 1 onion. Drain the lentils, put in a saucepan with the onion, bay leaf and water. Bring to the boil, reduce heat and simmer until the lentils are soft, then rub through a sieve or blend in a liquidiser.

Chop the remaining onion and the garlic. In a large saucepan, fry the chopped onion and garlic gently in *ghee* until soft. Add the garam masala and cook, stirring, for 2–3 minutes. Add the lentil purée, mix well, stir in the stock, season to taste, bring to the boil and simmer for a few minutes to heat through. Just before serving, blend in the coconut cream. Slice the lemon and serve separately.

Cod in Almond and Yogurt Sauce (page 66)

CURRIED FISH

SERVES 4

In India this recipe often uses local types of fish like pomfret or seer.

I kg/2 lb white fish fillet
I onion
2 cloves garlic
I–2 dried chillies
50 g/2 oz butter
I teaspoon ground coriander
½ teaspoon chilli powder
½ teaspoon turmeric
½ teaspoon ground mustard seed
I teaspoon rice flour
300 ml/½ pint coconut milk (page 74)
juice of ½ lemon
salt

Slice the fish into pieces. Chop the onion and garlic. De-seed and chop the chillies. Heat the butter, fry the onion until it softens and becomes transparent. Add the garlic, chilli and all the ground spices, stir and reduce heat. Dilute the rice flour with the coconut milk, pour the mixture into the pan and blend well. Add the lemon juice, season with salt to taste and simmer gently, stirring until the sauce thickens. Add the fish, make sure it is completely immersed in the sauce, simmer until tender and serve with rice.

COD IN ALMOND AND YOGURT SAUCE

SERVES 4

(Illustrated on previous page)

I kg/2 lb cod fillet
I teaspoon turmeric
salt and pepper
50 g/2 oz butter
4 onions
5-cm/2-in piece cinnamon stick
450 ml/¾ pint milk
225 g/8 oz ground almonds
150 ml/¼ pint natural yogurt

Wash and dry the fish fillets, cut into portions, dust with turmeric and season with salt and pepper.

Chop the onions, heat the butter in a saucepan, add the onion and cinnamon stick and cook gently until the onions soften. Add the cod, brown quickly, turn, then pour in the milk, let it reach boiling point, lower the heat and simmer gently for 15 minutes.

Pound the almonds in a mortar, moisten with yogurt, adding a little at a time, until you have a creamy paste. Pour over the fish, cover, simmer gently for 10 minutes and serve with boiled rice.

FISH PILAU

SERVES 6

675 g/1½ lb hake or cod fillets
350 g/12 oz long-grain rice
3 tablespoons ghee
I teaspoon turmeric
½ teaspoon ground coriander
I teaspoon garam masala (page 74)
pinch of chilli powder
I teaspoon salt
I tablespoon lemon juice
I large onion
900 ml/1½ pints hot water
225 g/8 oz peeled cooked prawns

Wash the fish, wipe with a cloth, and cut into six portions. Wash the rice and leave in water while preparing the other ingredients.

Heat half the ghee, add the turmeric, coriander, garam masala, chilli powder, and a good pinch of salt. Cook this spice paste for 2 minutes, moisten with lemon juice, then continue to cook over a fairly high heat, stirring all the time, until any surplus moisture evaporates. Add the fish and fry on both sides, allowing it to pick up as much of the spice mixture as will adhere, patting lightly with a fish slice. Be careful not to break the fish portions. Cook for 5 or 6 minutes and remove from pan.

Chop the onion. In a saucepan big enough to take all the ingredients, heat the rest of the *ghee* and fry the onion. Drain the rice, add to the saucepan, season with salt to taste, mix well and cook for 2 minutes. Add the pan juices left from frying the fish, mix well, then pour on the hot water and bring to the boil. Reduce heat, cover and cook gently for 20–25 minutes. Stir, arrange the fish on top of rice, cover, then continue to cook on a low heat for another 10 minutes. Garnish with prawns, replace cover, leave over gentle heat for 2–3 minutes and serve.

AK-NI KORMA

SERVES 4–5

'*Ak-ni*' is the Indian counterpart of the bouquet garni and consists of 1 tablespoon fennel seeds, 1 tablespoon coriander seeds and a small onion stuck with 2 cloves.

I Ak-ni *bouquet*
450–575 g| I–I¼ lb lean lamb
600 ml| I pint water
I medium onion
25 g| I oz butter
2½-cm| I-in piece cinnamon stick
2 cardamoms
I½ teaspoons salt
small pinch of cumin seed
300 ml|½ pint natural yogurt
½ teaspoon saffron strands

Tie the *ak-ni* ingredients in a muslin bag to facilitate removal from the saucepan before serving. Cut the meat into bite-sized cubes, put in a pan with the *ak-ni*, pour in the water and bring to the boil. Reduce heat, cover and simmer until the meat is tender and the liquid is reduced by two-thirds – about 45–50 minutes.

Fish Pilau (opposite)

Chop the onion. Heat the butter in a large saucepan, add and fry the onion. Add the remaining seasoning and spices, except saffron. Cook together for 2–3 minutes, stirring all the time. Dilute with yogurt, simmer for 7–8 minutes, then add the meat and the strained liquid in which it was boiled. Pound the saffron, then dilute it with a little of the cooking liquid. Pour the saffron liquid into the pan and blend well. Check seasoning, add more salt if necessary, and serve with rice, chutney and any side dishes you like.

CARDAMOM SPRING CHICKEN

SERVES 4

This famous dish came from the kitchens of the Mogul courts. Ideally it should be roasted on a spit. If you have to use the oven, make sure the bird is on a trivet in the roasting pan, above the pan juices. Only spring chicken is used for *Elachi murghi*.

2 spring chickens
salt
2 medium onions
100 g/4 oz butter
1 teaspoon ground cardamom
1 teaspoon black peppercorns
100 g/4 oz chicken livers
40 g/1½ oz fresh breadcrumbs

Wipe the chickens and rub with salt on the inside. Chop the onions, heat 3 tablespoons of the butter and fry the onion until it begins to soften. Add the cardamom and peppercorns, reduce heat and continue to cook, stirring, for 6–7 minutes.

Chop the chicken livers and add to the onion. Cook until they change colour. Season with salt to taste. Simmer for 7–8 minutes. Remove from heat, add the breadcrumbs, mix well, check seasoning, divide the mixture in half and stuff one portion into each chicken.

Brush the outside of the chickens with butter and roast for 35–40 minutes, basting with the remaining butter or pan juices from time to time.

DUCK VINDALOO

SERVES 4

Vindaloos are specialities of Southern India and are usually fiery. The amount of chillies for the vindaloo paste can be increased or decreased, depending on how hot you like your curry. Duck, goose and pork lend themselves particularly well to vindaloo recipes. If fresh lime juice is not available, use lemon juice or vinegar.

2–3 cloves garlic
2 medium onions
4 tablespoons butter
2 tablespoons vindaloo paste (see note below)
2 tablespoons lime juice
salt
4 duck joints
150 ml/¼ pint water

Chop the garlic and onions. Heat the butter and fry the garlic and onions until soft. Add the *vindaloo* paste and lime juice, simmer very gently for 5 minutes, taking care not to burn the mixture. Add the duck joints and salt to taste to pan, stir and pour in the water. Cover and simmer until tender – about 1 hour. Do not allow the juices to dry out; add more liquid if necessary, though it should not be needed if the heat is kept really low. Taste for seasoning and serve with rice.

Note on Vindaloo Paste: Put 5–6 deseeded fresh red chillies, 1-cm/½-in slice fresh root ginger (chopped), 1½ teaspoons ground coriander and 1 teaspoon ground cumin in a liquidiser. Add a little water and blend together to make a smooth paste, adding a little extra water as necessary.

Chapattis (page 72)

INDIAN MEATBALLS

SERVES 6

Indian meat balls – *kofta* – are made of minced beef or mutton, flavoured with chopped mint, onion, garlic, ginger, cinnamon, cardamom, and other spices, served in a curry sauce. They can also be made of fish, prawns and other shellfish, poached and reduced to a purée, then shaped into balls.

450 g / 1 lb beef
3 onions
3 cloves garlic
pinch of ground cinnamon
pinch of ground cardamom
pinch of ground cloves
salt and freshly ground black pepper
1 egg
flour or milk
2–3 tablespoons ghee
1–2 teaspoons garam masala (page 74)
600 ml / 1 pint coconut milk (page 74)
1 tablespoon lemon juice

Mince the beef finely. Chop one onion and one clove garlic. Add to the beef with the cinnamon, cardamom and cloves, season to taste with salt and pepper. Bind with the egg and mix well. Dipping your hands in flour or milk, shape the mixture into little balls, the size of a walnut. Fry them in hot *ghee* until light brown, remove with a slotted spoon, drain and leave the meatballs on one side.

Finely slice the remaining onions and garlic and fry in the *ghee* left in the pan. As soon as the onions become transparent, add the garam masala and fry, stirring, for 5 minutes. Gradually add the coconut milk and reduce heat so that the sauce simmers without boiling. Add the *kofta*, cover and simmer on lowest possible heat for 25–30 minutes, shaking the pan from time to time. Sprinkle with lemon juice and serve with rice.

Variation

Lamb kofta Proceed as above using minced lamb instead of beef and milk instead of coconut milk. Just before serving, gently blend into the sauce 2–3 tablespoons cream and sprinkle the top with grated nutmeg.

RICE WITH PEAS

SERVES 6

Vegetable pilaus are important in the diet of millions of Indians whose eating customs are dictated by religious regulations and taboos.

350 g / 12 oz rice
2 tablespoons ghee
4–5 cloves
2 cinnamon sticks
1 teaspoon caraway seeds
½ teaspoon turmeric
1½ teaspoons salt
350 g / 12 oz shelled peas
600 ml / 1 pint hot water

Wash the rice and leave covered with cold water for 45–50 minutes. Heat the *ghee* with the cloves, cinnamon, caraway seeds and turmeric, cook for 2–3 minutes on a very low heat, stirring all the time. Drain the rice, add to the fried spices and season with salt. Mix and fry together on a low heat for 5 minutes, stirring continuously. Add the peas and mix gently.

Add the water, increase heat and stir until the water comes to the boil. Reduce heat to low, cover and cook for 25–30 minutes.

VEGETABLE SAMOSAS

SERVES 4–6

This recipe originates in Bengal, but samosas are eaten all over India. Savoury samosas can have meat or vegetable fillings. In Northern India samosas are usually triangular or round, in the South they are crescent shaped. Savoury samosas with a lightly curried filling make excellent snacks and cocktail accompaniments.

175 g/6 oz plain flour
salt
4 tablespoons ghee
150 ml/¼ pint natural yogurt
I medium onion
I tablespoon coriander seeds
1½ teaspoons chopped fresh root ginger
½ teaspoon chilli powder
450 g/1 lb cooked mashed potato
I–1½ teaspoons garam masala (page 74)
I tablespoon lemon juice
2 teaspoons dried pomegranate seeds (optional)
I–2 tablespoons milk
fat or oil for deep frying

Sift the flour and a pinch of salt into a bowl, stir in 3 tablespoons of the *ghee* and the yogurt, knead gently into a dough, roll into a ball, cover with a bowl and leave to stand for 25–30 minutes while you prepare the stuffing.

Chop the onion. Pound the coriander seeds.

Heat the remaining *ghee* and lightly fry the onion to soften. Add the coriander seeds, ginger and chilli powder, stir and simmer for 2–3 minutes. Add the mashed potato, season to taste with salt and blend in the garam masala. Pound the pomegranate seeds (if used) and add to the potato mixture. Simmer on low heat to evaporate moisture – the stuffing should be on the dry side. Remove from heat and allow to cool.

Roll out the dough very thinly and cut into 5–7.5-cm/2–3-in squares, then put a generous teaspoon of the stuffing in each square, leaving the edges clear. Brush the edges with a little milk or water, fold corner to corner to make a triangle, and press well to seal the edges.

Heat the fat or oil and deep-fry a few samosas at a time until golden brown on both sides. Drain on absorbent kitchen paper and keep hot while you fry the remaining samosas. Serve with chutney.

Variation

Meat Samosas Follow the above recipe, substituting finely minced lamb or liver for potatoes and adding I minced clove garlic and I–2 peeled, chopped tomatoes to the stuffing.

VEGETABLE FRITTERS

MAKES 24

These *pakoras* are an Indian vegetarian version of the Japanese *tempura*. All sorts of vegetables are dipped in a batter made of *besom*, or split pea flour, flavoured with garam masala, then deep-fried a few at a time. You can use other vegetables – for example thinly sliced courgettes, aubergines or potatoes. Small sweet peppers can be used whole to make delicious *pakoras*.

225 g/8 oz split pea flour
250 ml/8 fl oz water
3 teaspoons salt
½ teaspoon turmeric
1½ teaspoons garam masala (page 74)
½ teaspoon chilli powder
I tablespoon dried pomegranate seeds (optional)
225 g/8 oz cauliflower
I–2 thin aubergines
oil for deep frying

Sift the flour into a bowl, very gradually add the water, stirring all the time until the batter reaches the consistency of thick cream. Leave to stand for half an hour. Season with 1½ teaspoons salt, add the turmeric and half the garam masala and chilli powder. Pound the pomegranate seeds, sprinkle into the batter and give it a good whisking.

Divide the cauliflower into florets. Slice the aubergine and drain off surplus liquid.

Mix the remaining salt, *garam masala* and chilli powder and set on one side.

Dip each piece of vegetable into batter just before frying. Heat the oil and deep fry a few *pakoras* at a time to prevent sticking. When golden brown, drain and sprinkle with the *garam masala* mixture. Serve piping hot with mint chutney.

AUBERGINE FOOGATH

SERVES 6

Foogaths are curried vegetable dishes, usually fried with spices and often cooked with fresh shredded coconut. These dishes are acceptable to all communities in all parts of India, irrespective of religious taboos. They can be served independently or as accompaniments to other curry dishes.

Aubergines, of which there are many varieties in India, are served in many ways, by themselves, or combined with other ingredients.

1 kg/2 lb aubergines
salt
3 medium onions
2 cloves garlic
2–3 tablespoons oil or ghee
1 tablespoon garam masala (page 74)
2 green peppers
1–2 dried chillies (optional)
pinch mustard powder
150 ml/¼ pint coconut milk (page 74)

Wash the aubergines, remove stems, but do not peel. Cut in uniform cubes, sprinkle with salt and leave to stand for 10–15 minutes. Pour off the bitter juices. Slice the onions finely and chop the garlic. Heat the oil or ghee and fry the onions and garlic until the onion becomes transparent and soft. Stir in the garam masala. Add the drained aubergine cubes and fry, stirring, for 1 minute. Deseed and dice the green peppers.

Deseed and pound the chillies. Add the peppers and chilli to the aubergine, check seasoning, adding more salt if necessary and add the mustard.

Moisten with the coconut milk, cover, reduce heat, then simmer on lowest possible heat for half an hour, without allowing the sauce to boil, and serve.

Aubergine Foogath

CHAPATTIS

MAKES 18–20

(Illustrated on page 69)

Chapattis are unleavened dough pancakes. They are served with curry and are a popular form of bread. In the North, wheat flour is used; in the South, rice flour is more common.

275 g/10 oz wholewheat flour
1 teaspoon salt
3 tablespoons vegetable oil
300 ml/½ pint warm water
2 tablespoons slightly warmed ghee

Reserve 50 g/2 oz flour for rolling out. Sift the remaining flour into a bowl, add the salt and oil, then gradually enough water to make a stiffish but pliable dough. Knead thoroughly. Wrap in a slightly dampened cloth and leave for an hour.

Knead the dough once more, then break into small pieces the size of a golf ball and roll lightly with floured hands. Flatten, then roll out into a pancake and, finally, toss the chapattis from hand to hand to make them thinner. Fry on a lightly greased hot griddle, or in a heavy-based frying pan. Allow about a minute each side. The frying must be done very quickly, otherwise the chapattis will become tough. When cooked they should be a very pale brown. Grease the griddle or pan after cooking each chapatti.

Brush each chapatti lightly with *ghee* on one side as soon as you remove it from heat, pile the chappatis on top of each other, cover with a napkin and keep warm in a low oven until they are all done.

PARATHA

MAKES 10

Paratha is a flaky type of Indian bread. Because parathas are impregnated with *ghee*, they should be served piping hot. Parathas are often filled with various vegetable mixtures, lightly curried potatoes, peas, cauliflower or *dhal*.

225 g/8 oz wholemeal flour
½ teaspoon salt
2 tablespoons oil
about 250 ml/8 fl oz water
100 g/4 oz ghee plus extra for cooking

Reserve 50 g/2 oz flour for shaping the bread. Use the remaining flour with the salt, oil and water to make the dough as for chappatis (above).

Divide the dough into 10 portions. Divide the ghee into 10 portions. Roll out each piece of dough, spread with *ghee*, fold and roll out again. Repeat the buttering, folding, and rolling process once or twice. (Indian cooks manage to do this without a rolling pin!).

Fry on a well greased griddle or in a heavy-based pan. As soon as one side is half cooked, turn and brush with *ghee*. Repeat on the other side. Cook until both sides are golden brown.

MANGO CHUTNEY

Chutney forms an essential part of an Indian meal. It is served with curry, or as an accompaniment to plain boiled rice – a spoonful of chutney goes a long way towards flavouring a helping of rice. In India it is usually made fresh daily and the Indian housewife, who doesn't normally possess a pestle and mortar, does her pounding and grinding most efficiently on a 'curry stone'. In affluent homes and restaurants several varieties of chutney are served with an Indian meal.

4 medium onions
4 mangos
3–4 bananas
225 g/8 oz sultanas
600 ml/1 pint malt vinegar
675 g/1½ lb sugar
1¼ teaspoon salt
¾ teaspoon pepper or chilli powder
1 teaspoon garam masala (page 74)
1 teaspoon mustard seeds

Slice the onions, mangos and bananas. Simmer with the sultanas in the vinegar for 45–50 minutes. Add the remaining ingredients, stir and continue to simmer for an hour. Cool, decant into jars and seal.

Variations

Apple Chutney As above, using apples instead of mangos.
Mixed Fruit Chutney An excellent chutney is made by following the instructions for Mango Chutney but using cooking apples, pears, peaches, plums and sultanas. To 1 kg/2 lb mixed chopped fruit allow 450 g/1 lb sugar and 450 ml/¾ pint vinegar. Add 6–8 minced cloves garlic, substitute caraway seeds for mustard seeds and cook the chutney on medium heat, stirring frequently for 45 minutes.

Mixed Fruit Chutney (opposite)

INDIAN COTTAGE CHEESE SWEEET

SERVES 4–6

450 g | 1 lb cottage cheese
pinch of saffron
2 tablespoons milk
450 g | 1 lb icing sugar
4–5 ground cardamom seeds
grated nutmeg

Make sure the cheese is well drained. Steep the saffron in the milk for half an hour.

Mix the cheese with the saffron flavoured milk, sugar and cardamom. Rub the mixture through a sieve or blend in a liquidiser. Transfer to a serving dish, sprinkle the top with nutmeg and serve chilled.

MANGO ICE CREAM

SERVES 6–8

Desserts, as the West know them, that is, sweet courses served after a meal, are not usual in India, though sweetmeats of all kinds are very popular.

3 egg yolks
350 ml | 12 fl oz milk
1 teaspoon vanilla essence
$\frac{1}{4}$ teaspoon salt
90 g | $3\frac{1}{2}$ oz sugar
225 g | 8 oz fresh or canned mangos
300 ml | $\frac{1}{2}$ pint double cream, whipped

Beat the yolks and add a small quantity of the milk. Scald the rest of the milk with the vanilla essences, salt and sugar and simmer gently until the sugar is completely dissolved. Remove from heat, blend gradually with the yolks, pour into a double saucepan, then cook over simmering water for a few minutes until the mixture thickens enough to coat the spoon. Remove from heat and continue to stir while the mixture cools. Slice the mangos and stir into the custard. Fold in the whipped cream, then freeze until slushy. Beat well, then return to the freezer until firm.

Glossary

Bamboo Shoots Available canned in large pieces or sliced from supermarkets.

Banana Leaves Large, thick glossy leaves which are sometimes used to serve food on. They are also used as a wrapping for foods before cooking in which case foil can sometimes be substituted. Available from ethnic and oriental stores.

Bean Curd White cakes of custard-like curd made from soya beans. Tasteless and takes on the flavour of ingredients with which it is cooked. Available from health food shops and oriental supermarkets either fresh (it is kept in water), in long-life packets or as a powder mix. Also known as tofu.

Blachan A strong paste made of pounded dried shrimps. Also known as blacan.

Bonito Fish This is a member of the tuna family. Sold dried in fine shavings, from oriental supermarkets and specialist Japanese stores. Used to make *dashi*, Japanese stock. Also known as *katsuobushi*.

Brown Soy Jam A thick dark brown paste made from soya beans and flavouring ingredients. Available from oriental supermarkets.

Cardamoms A mild spice with a delicate flavour. Whole cardamom pods are about the size of a peanut. Green are most common, white are quite expensive and brown are larger, hairy and not used as extensively. Used whole, or the small black seeds inside the pods are ground.

Chillies, fresh Green or red, in various shapes and varying degrees of hotness. Unless recipe states otherwise cut off stalk and remove seeds which are very hot. Wash hands thoroughly and avoid contact with eyes. Widely available.

Chinese Dried Mushrooms Similar in size to small field mushrooms but with a distinct flavour. Dark brown with pale middle. Soak in cold water for 15–30 minutes before use. Available from oriental supermarkets and good supermarkets. Also known as *shiitake*.

Chinese Wheat Starch Available only from oriental supermarkets. Plain flour or cornflour can be substituted.

Chinese Wine Far stronger than ordinary western wine, resembling fortified wines. Substitute dry sherry in cooking.

Coconut Cream/Milk Thick creamy liquid squeezed out of grated fresh coconut is the cream. Soaked in water, then squeezed again to obtain coconut milk. Desiccated coconut can also be used to make this milk. Packets of coconut cream in solid blocks can be diluted to make milk.

Coconut Water The liquid which is drained from the middle of fresh coconut.

Cinnamon Sticks About 5–7.5 cm/2–3 in long. Rolled bark of the cinnamon tree. Available as sticks and ground.

Coriander Seeds Small, round, pale seeds about the size of peppercorns. Also available ground. Widely available.

Coriander Leaves Grown from the seeds. They resemble tall, French parsley. Available from ethnic shops and good supermarkets.

Cumin Small, longish, black or pale seeds. Also available ground. Widely available.

Dried Shrimps Small, pinkish-brown, dried shrimps with a very strong smell and flavour. Used to make blachan. Must be washed and soaked before use. Available from oriental supermarkets.

Fermented Black Beans Small black beans with a very strong, salty taste. Available in packets, cans or jars from oriental supermarkets.

Five-spice Powder A strong Chinese flavouring powder made up of ground star anise, aniseed pepper, fennel, cloves and cinnamon. From oriental shops and in some supermarket ranges of oriental ingredients.

Garam Masala A ground Indian spice mixture consisting of cumin, coriander, cardamoms, cloves, peppercorns, mace, cinnamon, bay leaves and nutmeg. If the spice is prepared for individual dishes the ingredients and proportions vary. Many good-quality brands are available from supermarkets.

Ghee Clarified butter used extensively in Indian cooking. Available canned from ethnic shops or prepare your own by melting and simmering butter for about 15 minutes. Strain through muslin. The ghee will keep in a cool place for several months.

Ginger, fresh root Knobbly root with fairly thick skin (young very fresh ginger has a fine skin). Used sliced, shredded, grated or ground.

Widely available from supermarkets and greengrocers, it can be stored in a plastic bag in the refrigerator or buried in dry sand.

Ginger, preserved stem From delicatessens and good supermarkets, tender stem ginger in syrup.

Gingko Nuts Small white nuts, slightly larger than peanuts. Canned or dried from oriental supermarkets.

Harusame Noodles Japanese noodles made from potato starch or soya bean starch. Available from Japanese specialist stores and some oriental supermarkets.

Hoisin Sauce A sweetish, strong, brown sauce made from soya beans, flavoured with garlic, chillies and other spices. Widely available.

Japanese Fish Cakes Red and white coloured cakes of ground fish available from Japanese specialist shops. Also known as _kohaku kamaboko_.

Lemon Grass A grass native to Asia. Coarse, reed-like but short with a lemon flavour. Available from oriental and ethnic shops also from good supermarkets. Also known as _serah_ or _serai_.

Mustard Seeds Small hot seeds which can be dark or light in colour.

Nam Pla Fermented fish sauce with a strong flavour. Available from oriental shops. Substitute I tablespoon anchovy paste mixed with I tablespoon soy sauce.

Noodles, Chinese egg Thin, yellow noodles available dried from most supermarkets. Require brief cooking in boiling water.

Noodles, rice Thin, flat noodles made from rice flour. Cut into strips which are about 25–30 cm/10–12 long.

Noodles, transparent Very fine transparent noodles, similar to vermicelli.

Nori Dried Japanese seaweed. Sold dried in very thin sheets which change colour when waved over a gas flame or electric ring. Available from specialist shops.

Oyster Sauce A brown sauce made from oysters, soy sauce and salt. Available from oriental shops and in some oriental ranges sold in good supermarkets.

Palm Sugar Raw, rich dark brown sugar sold in compressed cakes. Substitute dark brown sugar. Also known as jaggery.

Peanut Oil Widely available, also known as groundnut oil.

Plum Sauce A sweet, thick Chinese sauce available bottled from good supermarkets and oriental shops.

Pomegranate Seeds Small, hard, black-red seeds. Sold dried in oriental supermarkets and ethnic shops.

Rice Vinegar Vinegar made from rice wine. Available from Japanese stores: also known as _su_.

Saffron The bright yellow stigmas of a crocus, this expensive spice contributes a delicate flavour and bright colour. Available as strands or powdered. Strands must be pounded, then dissolved in hot water.

Sake Japanese rice wine. Served warmed as a drink. It has a nutty flavour. Also used in cooking. Available from oriental shops.

Sesame Oil Strongly flavoured, light or dark in colour. Available from health food shops and good supermarkets.

Sesame Paste A smooth, thick and oily paste made from ground unroasted sesame seeds. Available from health food shops and oriental supermarkets.

Soy Sauce Widely available, dark or light. Use Japanese soy sauce (from Japanese shops) for Japanese dishes.

Tamarind Dark black pods compressed into cakes. Soaked and squeezed out to yield a tart liquid. Available as tamarind juice or paste. From oriental and ethnic shops.

Turmeric A bright yellow spice. Widely available.

Water Chestnuts Widely available canned.

White Radish Large long radish similar in size to a thin parsnip. Used in Japanese cooking. Available from good supermarkets. Also known as _mooli_ and _daikon_.

Wun Tuns Chinese dumplings, made from a thinly rolled egg dough which is cut into squares and filled with a meat mixture.

Index